MISSING PIECES

My hope is that you
receive healing, peace,
and an abundance of all
good things!

Keep going... You'll Rise up!

With Gratitude,
Andi Hunt

MISSING PIECES

When We Don't Understand the Darkness,
We Can't Find a Path to the Light

Andi Hunt

NEW DEGREE PRESS

COPYRIGHT © 2021 ANDI HUNT

MISSING PIECES

When We Don't Understand the Darkness,
We Can't Find a Path to the Light

ISBN

978-1-63730-649-9   *Paperback*

978-1-63730-732-8   *Kindle Ebook*

978-1-63730-923-0   *Digital Ebook*

I dedicate this book to the person who taught me:

How to dance like nobody is watching.

How to crotchet.

How to be silly.

How to be adventurous, even when you're scared.

The joy of sitting on a porch swing.

To love the ocean.

How amazing bare feet feel in cool spring grass.

That good accessories can bring an outfit together.

The simplicity of a good homegrown garden.

When to hold my tongue and know when to speak up.

How to be kind to others even when they haven't been kind to me.

How to forgive.

Not to fear change or new things.

That I can do anything I set my mind to.

How to be resourceful and make something out of nothing.

How to represent your best self to the world.

How to listen when someone just needs to be heard.

The power of music on good days and bad, especially Elvis songs.

How to love people even through their worst times.

How important family is.

The importance of being present for someone when they are struggling, even when there aren't sufficient words of comfort.

How to leave a legacy when my spirit goes to be with the Lord.

Nana, this is for you.

CONTENTS

———

"I've learned that people will forget what you said, people will forget what you did, but people will never forget how you made them feel."

—MAYA ANGELOU

A NOTE FROM THE AUTHOR

———

Dear Reader,

As far back as I can remember, I've been afraid of the dark. Darkness is simply the absence of light, proven to me countless times when my parents turned on the light to check my room for monsters. However, that knowledge didn't stop me from fearing what I couldn't see. I would curl up in a ball under my comforter every night at bedtime. Little did I know the real monsters came out in broad daylight, in plain sight. The devil doesn't always look like the devil, which is hard lesson to learn at such a young age.

The light and bright parts of my life were a set of amazing and loving parents, grandparents, great-grandparents, and a load of aunts, uncles, and cousins. With my family and extended family, we had cookouts, campouts, and gatherings for holidays; we played sports and had a great time. From the outside looking in, our family was just fine. Through the years I've also had a handful of trusted friends that were there for me during the dark times in my life, even though they didn't know the truth about what I had been through. For those friends, I'll be forever grateful.

Despite all the light times, darkness began to seep into my life when I was five years old. I was taught to sneak around, hide, lie, and do what I was told by someone who was very persuasive. The first monster was a little girl who was a few years older than me. She sexually abused me for two years, doing things to me that a girl her age shouldn't have known about. She would lock me in the bathroom at her house or a storage building and refused to let me out until I let her do what she wanted. I didn't understand why she wanted to do these dirty things to me, but I understood her when she said, "Don't ever tell anyone the things *we* did or we'll both be in big trouble." In my young mind, being in trouble meant going to jail. My daddy was a police officer, and I *never* wanted to be in trouble with him or my mother. So, I kept my secrets for most of my life. Or did they keep me?

As a result of being locked in a bathroom and various other places, I developed a fear of confined spaces and not being in control of an event or situation. I was older and my monsters were transforming into buried secrets and feelings of being trapped, like I had no value. This must have been apparent outwardly as I became a prime target for bullies and panicked at the thought of being held anywhere without an escape plan.

Still, I had no professional help. I never saw a counselor as a child. It wasn't something my family or friends discussed because they didn't know anything was wrong. I never told my parents what happened to me. If I had told them they would've done whatever it took to help me. My mind locked those memories up like Fort Knox and it became my unrealized cage, a confined space and feeling. Subconsciously, I would scan a room as I entered it looking for the potential dangers, a.k.a. bullies: a co-worker who didn't like me, or literally anything that my brain saw as a threat. It was exhausting. No matter where I went, who I was with, or what I was doing, I was in constant fight-or-flight mode.

I ran from my trauma for thirty-eight years. I know exactly how it feels to be insecure, to have the nagging desire to be included, to engage in negative self-talk and view one-self with a distorted image. I know all too well the feelings of shame, guilt, crippling anxiety, and panic progressing to the point of losing my voice. I knew what I wanted to say, but when I tried every word came out with an "-ing" on the end of it. It was like wires got crossed in my brain. If I didn't stop talking, lie down, and focus on breathing, it would increase in intensity to the point I couldn't string a sentence together in my mind, let alone try to say it. For as long as I can remember I felt like I was flawed. I tried different antianxiety medica-tions, a new one every couple of years, starting when I was twenty. I drank to mask the pain. After a while, gambling became my mind-numbing distraction. And when all that didn't work, I became suicidal. I thought, *This world would be better off without me in it.* It makes my heart break a little every time I think back to those times I said that to myself.

I desperately wanted a more calm and peaceful life, and I'd often wonder what my calling in life was. I knew I wanted to help people, yet unsure in what way. My calling presented itself to me in July 2020, in the middle of a global pandemic. Every sermon I watched online, motivational speech I heard, or life coach podcast I listened to seemed to give specific encouragement for me, to *write the book!* Repeated confirmation came every day for two weeks. While checking the *Farmers' Almanac* for *best days* to cut your hair to promote growth, I ran across a *best day* that stood out in bold to me: **Write!**

I had become in tune with listening to God and being obedient, so I began.

I prayed over sharing my story, having faith my mental state would be transformed, to turn my pain into power, and encourage others to seek healing the way I had been dreaming of. As the words began to flow, I realized I couldn't accomplish this task until I found a path to healing for myself, so I reached out to a friend the same day, who recommended a counselor.

I began seeing my counselor sometimes twice a week in July 2020 and haven't stopped. She was certified in EMDR therapy, Eye Movement Desensitization and Reprocessing. It helped me recover the missing pieces of my childhood. I was able to unlock memories I wasn't even aware I had. Once, at twenty-five, I had one session of EMDR and didn't know enough about it at that time to realize it takes consistent work to get better. I thought since I'd uncovered the memory that was causing me such grief, I could handle the recovery on my own. Yet at forty-three I was desperate to feel better, BE better, and have the life I wanted and deserved. I was motivated to go through the dark parts to get to the light. To the other side. Recovery.

After nearly three decades of my monsters having control over my life, I yanked the chain that connected us, looked them dead in the eye and said, "I'm sick of this and I AM TAKING MY LIFE BACK!"

Some of my secrets were buried so deep it took me nearly nine months to dig them up through EMDR therapy, process them in my adult brain, and have the ability to move forward.

After being fully committed to getting the help I needed, it was as if the darkness had no place in my life anymore. The light began to outweigh the dark. I saw things, events, and memories, through fresh eyes. I felt in my spirit I was on the right path to fulfill my divine calling.

The energetic draw was intense to commit to writing this book (*and, yes, you can opt out of your calling*). I started to talk about my adverse childhood experiences. Little did I know that sharing my unfolding story would take me to such a vulnerable place. I wasn't accustomed to allowing myself to be vulnerable in my adult life. I felt I had to control everything, stay busy constantly, or mask the pain somehow. I began dipping my toe into the waters of vulnerability by telling family, close friends, and then acquaintances about my healing journey, which led to sharing my trauma and the aftereffects of it. What I began to see was that there are many people just like me who have buried a negative, hurtful memory. An experience that seems impossible even to reach, much less to heal from.

I am now in my early forties, and after publicly announcing the creation of my first book, I've had people ages thirty-five to sixty share their childhood and adult traumas with me. What I've learned is that no matter the trauma, it doesn't go away unless you are intentional about changing your life for the better.

My hope is to encourage every person who either has an unhealed trauma, or knows someone who does, to seek counseling, therapy, and recovery. This book is for anyone who has experienced panic, anxiety, addiction, or PTSD, or who knows someone who has experienced them.

After everything I've been through, I wouldn't change a thing about my life, not even the dark parts. There have been many lighter and more beautiful, funny, and wonderful times. My story has made me the person I am today and has propelled my purpose to shine a light into the darkness, like a lighthouse in the fog, for others who may be lost.

Together, we can chart a destination to healing, one person at a time.

CHAPTER 1

THE HOUSE
ALWAYS WINS

———

In the spring of 2012, I was able to purchase a new car off the showroom floor. It was a big accomplishment for me, since I'd never earned six figures before. I named my car Pearl. She was a bright white four-door Scion with fairy dust sparkles in the paint. It's strange to think about the contrast now, because she was so white and pure in color, but I felt so dark and gloomy inside. I still have her today, nine years later.

Several years after getting my symbol of accomplishment, in my mid-thirties, I drove Pearl to my favorite casino. Pulling into the dimly lit underground parking garage felt eerie. Maybe I had watched too many episodes of *CSI*. Nothing good ever happens in that show, especially in the bowels of a parking garage. I began scanning the area for any vehicles I might recognize. My head swiveled, constantly checking for cars pulling in through the entrance nearby or circling for an open parking spot. I had to be *sure* no one saw or recognized me. I couldn't take the risk of being caught because my husband and family simply couldn't know I was doing this. I learned to park underground to avoid the greatest risk of being seen.

My gambling addiction was innately tied to my childhood trauma, but I didn't know this at the time. I only knew I had to keep this secret at all costs. If I was caught, I would let down the people I loved most in my life since I'd promised time and time again I'd never go back to gambling. Hiding, lying, and keeping secrets had been part of my life since I was five years old. I was a seasoned expert.

Once I'd found a secure and well-hidden spot to park, I would make my way to the glass-enclosed entrance decorated with two benches, a ficus tree in each corner, and a tall outdoor ashtray bin. I recognized the familiar smell of gasoline and oil-covered asphalt as I reached for the door handle. All my senses were heightened while I continued to check over both of my shoulders for any sign of someone I might know. When I opened the glass doors, there it was. The faint scent of cigarette and cigar smoke mixed with some type of air freshener or odor neutralizer. It was a distinct smell. It told me I was closer to where I wanted to be, and that made me feel soothed somehow. I would rush to the elevator and push the up button.

Entering the casino, my heart started thumping faster as soon as I caught a glimpse of the intoxicating atmosphere, its deep purple carpet luring me into the ocean of sparkling slot machines and sharply dressed gamblers softly mumbling to their companions, hoping, like me, to leave with more money than they had come with.

This seemingly beautiful, alluring haven was where I located my rock bottom. It's where I lost nearly everything. The house always wins in the end. My sense of control over my life, my home, and many relationships finally brought me to realize I needed to seek therapy and share my truth. A truth that had to first be told to my mother.

After many hours of researching trauma and the significant adverse effects it can have on a person, I took my first steps into the unknown world of vulnerability. I had to tell my mother what happened to me as a child.

It was on an evening during the first week of October 2020. As the sun was setting, I went out into my driveway and sat on the tailgate of my husband's truck. We were in the middle of a global pandemic, so I couldn't see my mother in person to tell her the secrets I'd kept for so long. I had to call her. It was probably better this way. I'm not sure I could've held my emotions together in person. The day prior I had texted her to ask her for a time when we could talk on the phone, in private. She knew I was going to tell her something significant, so she was anxiously awaiting my call.

I'm extremely close to my mom and I was convinced this news would come as a shock to her, so when she answered, and I was able to remove my heart from my vocal cords: I said hello. I asked about her day, and she commented that it was fine, but she was more worried about what I needed to tell her. With not a calm nerve in my body, I began to tell her the reason for my call.

"Mom. I wrote a letter to you so I can keep my train of thought and be able to make it through it. Please let me read it to you. Then I'll answer any questions you have." I exhaled. My mom went quiet, and I began to read.

Dear Mom,

Do you remember when you had to drive me to see my therapist when I was twenty-five? Coby was still a baby in his carrier car seat, and Tori was in kindergarten. That day, I remember thinking,

"I can't do this." As you always do, you encouraged me and said, "I am right here with you, and you can do this because I will never leave you." I felt so weak, scared, and sick to my stomach, like my heart would beat straight out of my chest. Well, that therapist was able to help me remember things I had been suppressing for twenty years with EMDR therapy. I thought I could fix myself and didn't realize I needed to continue EMDR therapy to get better, versus other forms of therapy. The number of other counselors I've had over the eighteen years since the first treatment have all suggested I tell you what happened to me as a child. After three months of the specific therapy, I needed to process my sexual abuse. I've finally healed enough to talk about it.

Thirty-eight years ago, I was molested for a span of about two years, starting at the age of five. It was someone I thought was my friend. She was the daughter of one of your friends. I never wanted to tell you because I feared I'd be in trouble, because she always threatened me not to tell or we would both be in trouble and couldn't play together anymore.

I never wanted to share this with you, even as an adult, because I didn't want this news to leave you burdened, hurt, or feeling guilty for not protecting me. I want you to know this was not your fault. I had the most amazing childhood because of you, Dad, Nana, and Papa. I realized at twenty-five years old that you had no indication something like that happened to me.

Now I know the devil doesn't always look like the devil.

The first time it happened, I recall her taking me to a tin shed. It had windows and I remember the sunshine coming through and bouncing off all the shiny things and the concrete floor. She did things to me I realized in my late twenties a girl her age would not have known to do, unless she'd been abused as well. There were many times after that. One time, you let me go out in our backyard to play on my swing set and you told me to stay there where you could see me from the kitchen window while you finished preparing dinner.

It was getting close to dusk. Jessica lived behind our house, across a little field. She came over to our yard and asked me to come to her house and play. She led me inside the house so quickly I don't remember what the living room or kitchen looked like. She took me straight to the bathroom and locked the door. I do remember the sudden banging on the bathroom door by her mom, yelling, "Jessica! Open this door!" It shocked me, and then I heard you say, "Andi, are you in there? Open this door!" in a worried voice, which made me even more scared. She held her pointer finger up to her mouth, and she mouthed the words, "Be quiet." She wasn't finished with me. I knew you were just on the other side of that door, and I was relieved. But she kept going. I'm not sure how long it was, but I remember hearing you and her mother continuing to yell, "Unlock this door!"

She finally let me out and I remember walking home holding your hand and you saying, "You scared me to death! I was so worried about you. Why did you leave the yard?" I don't remember what I said, but I could feel how much you truly and unconditionally loved me. You always made me feel that way and still do.

Again, I am grateful for the childhood I had and for having you and Dad as parents. You taught me what is important, like being kind to one another, asking about the other person's day, always showing affection by giving hugs when you see family or friends, being honest and trustworthy, having a solid work ethic, and, most of all, loving everyone equally. I wouldn't change my childhood, even if I could go back and erase the bad parts. I am too grateful for the good.

With Love and Gratitude,
Andi

It was quiet for a few seconds as my mother gathered her thoughts and found her opportunity to interject with a question, which she is lovingly notorious for. She asked,

"Well, this puts a black mark on it, don't you think?"

I laughed, a relieved kind of laugh as if this was the first breath I'd taken since beginning the call. This was her first comment after this news I'd held in for thirty-eight years for fear of hurting her. I said, "Absolutely NOT!" I reassured her by reiterating how much my childhood truly meant to me. I shared some of my favorite memories with her and we laughed together, reminiscing about old times.

I continued, "I realize this is a lot of information and it may take you a while to process your feelings, thoughts, and emotions. You don't need to feel obligated to say anything immediately. However, if you have questions, I'm happy to answer them."

"Honey, her mom was my best friend. I had known her practically my entire life and never had a single thought something like that was going on, especially with Jessica," Mom replied.

"When you and dad bought the new house, I didn't see Jessica anymore. I didn't know why and never thought to ask where she went. I just knew there would be no more of her dirty games."

After that, in my eight-year-old brain, her memory dissipated like a spring fog after the sunlight warmed up the land. I could tell my mom was in shock, but she was handling it well. She didn't ask for details. As a mom myself, I doubt I would immediately ask for details. I suppose you never know until faced with something similar. It is a lot of information that seems unreal and unbearable. Even though it was practically a lifetime ago, that doesn't stop a mother's guilt, and the way we second-guess our maternal instincts. I feel like my babies, Coby and Tori, will always be my babies no matter their ages. I can only imagine what must have been going through my mother's mind at the time I read this letter to her.

Knowing she should take some time to continue to process this information, I asked her to call me if she had questions. I told her I loved her, and I would talk to her soon. As I was hanging up the phone, a feeling of regret hit me. I wished I had told her when I was five or even twenty-five. I could've had all those years in a healed state and not on a mental and emotional roller coaster. I lived for over three decades trying to cover up and mask the pain. Hindsight is 20/20. My trauma led me on a path filled with hurt, addiction, negative self-talk, distorted self-image, and risky behavior.

Every time I tried a new counselor, therapist, or psychiatrist I was disappointed. I went into each appointment with hope and a desperation to feel better. They all wanted to know what anti-anxiety or antidepressant medication I'd already tried so they could recommend or prescribe me a new pill to stitch up my hemorrhaging mental state. As they sat scribbling down a note or entering information into their computer, I sat there in a hopeless daze, thinking, *Find another way to fix me. I will not ever tell my mother those gruesome things. I don't want her to be burdened by the guilt of knowing. It was not her fault, and I won't do that to her. She's too good a mother and my love for her is more intense than the pain.*

I tried to white-knuckle my way through every time I was triggered into a fight-or-flight response. The pieces were all in the box, but the box had no picture. I had to figure out how to put them together to heal. After obsessive hours of research, I learned that unprocessed trauma can cause addiction (gambling), acting impulsively (buying a car off the showroom floor), or shame or guilt (not wanting to tell my mother about my trauma). Once I embraced the fact that I had to DO something I was uncomfortable with, I learned being comfortable with being uncomfortable was part of the journey. The road has been a long, steep climb.

Thankfully, through the experience of therapy, I have learned the truth always bubbles up to the surface to find a way out of the darkness and into the light.

CHAPTER 2

NIGHT AND DAY

———

My parents were high school sweethearts. They married and bought a single wide mobile home in my mom's hometown. I grew up in that small northern Oklahoma town with one four-way stop, three churches, a post office, a tiny gas station, a couple of little stores, and a bar. The town was small in the early eighties. The population was around 450 people, but I highly suspect someone counted the cows and horses. At around eight years old, I rode my bicycle over every street in that town. It was a pale yellow, banana seat bicycle with streamers in the handles. There wasn't a day I didn't leave home without my long brunette hair fixed in pigtail braids. They swung from side to side as I lifted off the seat to pedal faster. I felt like I was flying and had not a solitary care.

In 1985, when I was eight, my parents upgraded and bought a house in the same town. That house. Woo-wee! The new house felt like a mansion to me! It was a three-bedroom, two-bath, rock-finished house with a little nook in the bottom of the linen closet. It was just big enough for me to crawl in with one of my mom's lamps to color and draw. I had my own little built-in fort without the hassle of turning kitchen chairs upside down and using sheets. The house had four big trees lining the circle driveway. I had a big bedroom and a trampoline in the backyard. I thought, *We're rich!*

We had dinner at the kitchen table nearly every evening. My mom always had dinner ready when my dad got home from work. My parents would talk about their days at work, and we'd giggle about something funny Dad said. He was quite a character and my hero. My mom was like an angel to me. I was mesmerized by her hair, her makeup, always a frosted light pink lipstick, and trendy tops. She was so kind and friendly to everyone.

I was drawn to helping dad with his flip projects too. He'd buy a truck, car, or motorcycle to fix it up and sell it. He'd earn a few extra bucks, then use part of the money to go buy something different and repeat the process. When he was working on his latest project, I went out to assist by handing him tools and asking him no less than one thousand questions. I learned a lot of modified cuss words when I was helping him. Mom didn't favor that, but she'd just get onto him in her conservative way. After a sale of one of these flips, we'd all venture out to dinner as a family. We usually went to a pizza place in a nearby town. One of my favorite places had arcade games and a great big jukebox. A dollar's worth of quarters would get you several games on each machine and a little knickknack out of the trinket machines—complete bliss to me at that age.

There was no alcohol in my home. Nobody ever said, "Hey, the rule is we shall have no alcohol in this house!" My parents simply didn't drink. We got six channels on the TV on a good day, so we didn't watch it much. However, nearly every memory I have with my parents and my grandparents was filled with music playing lightly in the background, unless it was a Saturday. Saturdays were the day my mother and I cleaned the house. If it was above fifty degrees outside, mom would open the windows, give me some menial tasks like dusting and vacuuming, and we'd turn the radio up loud to listen to the top forty country countdown. Music always had a happy memory intertwined with it.

When I stayed with my maternal grandmother, Nana, we would sing and dance to country or Elvis. She loved Elvis. And I loved her. She was thoughtful, spunky, full of energy, and had a fierce light that you wanted to warm up to. She and my maternal grandfather, Popsie, grew a huge garden every summer full of cantaloupe, cucumbers, tomatoes, and okra. She'd fry or boil the okra, cut up the other veggies, add some kind of protein, and serve cantaloupe for dessert. On those days, the window unit air conditioner fought to keep up with the humid Oklahoma summer heat. Sometimes after dinner Popsie would teach me an easy song on the piano and they'd cheer for me like they'd never seen such a talented child.

Nana worked at the school I attended, so when I was around, most of the kids would call her Nana too. She was like everyone's fill-in grandmother at school. Eventually, my mother got a job at my school too. That meant she didn't have to drive to the city an hour away. I could see Mom or Nana anytime I wanted to. It was a comfort through my transition from a tomboy to a young woman. I naturally got along better with boys because I didn't fancy the dolls, dresses, and bows. I never owned a Barbie doll. I preferred playing in the dirt, running barefoot through the grass, climbing trees, and riding my bike.

I had one teacher all day in third grade, and her name was Mrs. Strawberry. She was about four feet, five inches tall, wore a perfectly coiffed grey beehive, and always clasped her hands together under her hefty bosom. I enjoyed being in her class and everyone knew that when you visited her house on Halloween, she gave out canned soda. Everyone hurried to get to her house before they were all gone. I was already taller than Mrs. Strawberry by the end of third grade. There were only about ten other students in my class, and they started to pick up on the fact that I was outgrowing them, especially the boys. By this time, at nine years old, I had just enough chest to cause need for the dreaded first bra. I was mortified, because one little boy would pop my strap from behind and the other kids would laugh in response.

By then, I'd outgrown the fear of the imaginary monsters hiding under my bed or in my closet. The memory of Jessica and the sexual abuse had been tucked so far back in my brain that I had forgotten about it. However, a new monster presented herself. Her name was Ravyn. Her name meant darkness, which I knew by looking it up in a baby name book my mom had. She was the polar opposite of what my Nana would call sweet-natured. Rayvn began to relentlessly bully me, for reasons unknown to me. She would invite me over to mimic music videos choreography with a few other girls around our age. She'd act like we were friends, but in the middle of one of our dance routines, she'd make a face at me that looked like she'd eaten a bug and say, "What was *that* move?"

"That's what they're doing in the video. Isn't it?"

She would smirk again and get the others to join in with her making fun of my moves. Ravyn learned that by making fun of me in the classroom she could fire the whole class up in laughter at my expense. The other kids caught on, so they would join in or start the daily routine of verbal and mental torture. The boys started to invite her to go horseback riding or fishing. This attention from the boys only fueled her fire to exclude me. I was singled out every single day of school. She or one of the boys would start making fun of my last name and they came up with some that would send me home crying and miserable after the bell rang. I tried my best to ignore it and not show that she was getting the better of me, because that's what my parents and grandparents told me to do.

I would begin dreading school on Sundays, knowing I had to face Ravyn again at school and during sports practice. I would get hot and sweaty, my heart would race, and I'd immediately be nauseous. At that time my mom or Nana would call it a nervous stomach. She didn't use anything but her words to hurt me. Whoever coined the phrase about sticks and stones never met Rayvn. I was miserable for most of fifth, sixth, and seventh grade.

Over the summer between seventh and eighth grade, I began to care about what I looked like. I sat and practiced makeup at a mirror in my bedroom, sometimes multiple times in one night, with my favorite eighties music blaring. I hadn't seen any of the boys from my class over the summer. When I walked into my class on my first day of eighth grade, I turned heads. There was something different about the way I carried myself. I was pretty. I was getting compliments from the boys my age and Ravyn would snarl her nose and glare at me. She wasn't getting all their attention anymore, so she turned the bullying up a notch. She started inviting people over to her house for parties and purposefully left me out. I'd hear about it from someone that was there or that heard about the party. She would spread rumors about me doing dirty things to some older boys. I didn't even know what the slang sexual terms meant. It still bothered me, but I tried not to let her see that. My mom and Nana would say,

"Honey, she's just jealous of you. Ignore her and that will upset her more than if you react to her nonsense."

I could not figure out why she would be jealous of me. I thought I was ugly and grotesque up until the boys noticed how much I'd morphed from a tomboy to what they then described as "really pretty." I may have been considered pretty on the outside, but it didn't mirror the ugliness I felt inside. I had a horrible habit of negative self-talk about my body, my hair, my face shape, my nose, my everything. I felt a darkness inside I couldn't explain. I knew I wasn't good enough to be valued by anyone but my family.

Then came Dawn. My one and only true friend. She and I became incrementally closer from fifth grade and on. Between seventh and eighth grade, we became inseparable. Dawn was a blue-eyed, natural blond with mid-length hair and bangs ratted about four inches tall and heavily sprayed with Aqua Net. She had a pale complexion, but her high energy and the way she'd tell a story was anything but. You could hear her laugh a block away. Dawn was the feeling of outward positivity, with such a big smile you felt like you can see her wisdom teeth. She wore eighties-style wire-rimmed glasses, and she always had them on. She had my back. Even though she was older, she still lived in the same town I lived in, and we saw each other often. If she heard someone mouth off about me, she'd say,

"Excuse ME? Were you just saying something? Don't whisper it, say it so we can all hear it!"

She was very vocal in her thoughts and feelings, like it or not, but she was one of the most kind and thoughtful people I knew.

Dawn was a quick-witted, intelligent girl with an exceptional memory. I knew if she was telling a story, it was truthful and never void of detail. Dawn would invite me over for sleepovers and concerts. I would invite her over to swim in the summers. She made me feel *included* and *wanted* as a friend, with no strings attached. During the times when Rayvn was bullying me, Dawn was always a safe place and a friend I could count on. Dawn never left me out of anything. On the days when I would come home crying after school because of Rayvn's incessant tormenting, I could call Dawn and she'd cheer me up by saying something silly about Rayvn. She did it to show me that Ravyn wasn't perfect and I wasn't as ugly and awful as I felt. She'd tell me so.

"YOU are NOT ugly. She is an immature brat and she's just jealous of you."

There's that phrase again, I'd think, *She's just jealous of you.* My mind wouldn't let me believe it.

After some time of seeing what Rayvn was putting me through, Dawn said to me, "I asked my mom if I could go and have a talk with Rayvn to ask why she was so mean to you and tell her she better leave you alone. But Mom said to be there for you and let the drama with Rayvn go." I replied with, "Why? It's not fair that she's mean to Andi for no reason."

"There are reasons that you don't need to know about, so help Andi brush it off and just be a good friend to her."

I often wondered what those *reasons* were, because Rayvn was relentless in her verbal and mental attacks. What would make her that mean? And why was she so mean to ME?

Rayvn and Dawn were like night and day. With Dawn I could be myself. I could act goofy or be creative and not be shamed or bullied or go home crying. I cherished my time spent with Dawn and her younger sister Emily. Emily was a year younger than me, but it was mostly the three of us in the beginning. Dawn was there for me, with me, and got me through some really dark times. She would typically ask me to come over for a sleepover, at least one night out of every weekend. Dawn always wanted to watch the movie *Grease* she had recorded on a VHS tape or the weekly pop video countdown that aired late at night on Fridays and Saturdays. We were eighties preteens and grew up with Rubik's cubes, tube bracelets with water and glitter inside, neon stretchy bracelets, Swatches (if you were "rich," you had them in all colors and stacked them from your wrist to your elbow), Z Cavaricci, Guess, Girbaud jeans, and cheer shorts in bright colors with hideous geometric shapes or tropical prints. We loved eighties pop, country, and rock music, the hair, and the movies.

We memorized every single phone number of the people in our circle of friends and family. As we got older, she and I were lucky enough to get teenage phone lines, separate lines our parents added on to their service to avoid hearing the phone ring every two minutes. We played outside, jumped on trampolines, swam in our pool, played softball and basketball, and rode our bikes or walked all over town together. We had one consistent rule with all our parents: be home before the streetlights come on.

Sprinkled in with all the sunshine filled days, there were a couple of times that I distinctly remember calling Dawn on her private phone line when I was feeling full of self-hate and worthlessness, wishing I could just disappear. One night, when I was thirteen, I called Dawn and told her,

"I don't want to live anymore."

After we hung up, she was at my door within ten minutes. It was only about 10:30 p.m., during the summer, but a work night for our parents. My room was dark, except a black light that my mom gave me from her youth. The radio was on low, playing eighties rock ballads. She joined me on the comforter pallet I'd made in my bedroom floor.

I started to cry,

"Why are you even friends with me? I don't deserve to have friends."

The feeling of despair was intense. I wanted to disappear. Vanish. Escape. I was in a level of internal darkness that I couldn't seem to pull myself out of on my own, and I didn't understand why.

Dawn's mouth gaped open, and she looked confused and hurt. She began to cry.

"Why would you say that? I love you and you are a great friend and person. You have no idea how much that hurts me to hear you say such a thing."

I turned away from her and cried. She continued reassuring me how much I meant to her and encouraged me to forget about whatever was bothering me, whether it was Ravyn or something else. She stayed up with me until the early morning hours talking and trying to change the mood to funny stories. It worked. Dawn's unwavering friendship and ability to make me laugh when I wanted to die was one of the reasons I made it through that time in my life. She helped make me a better person by showing me what real friends do for each other.

I began to realize the negative feelings I had didn't start with Rayvn and her bullying. It started much before that. I just couldn't figure out what it was. My internal line of questioning went something like this,

"Am I ugly? Is it because I'm not cool? Why do I feel more comfortable when I am alone? What is wrong with me?"

Once I graduated from eighth grade, I had to choose between a few different high schools nearby. One was rather small and the other was quite large in comparison to what I was used to in class size. I chose the latter. Dawn went to another school. She and I had an awesome summer, and I didn't have to see Ravyn. Every night I lay in bed with the radio playing in the background and pondered how my freshman year of high school would be without Dawn. *Would Ravyn be there, like a dark hovering cloud I couldn't shake?*

CHAPTER 3

YOU'LL ALWAYS BE MY LITTLE GIRL

———

I was quite a basketball player from fifth through eleventh grade. I loved the game. Dad and I used to practice in the driveway. He helped coach our teams when I was younger. When I started playing softball, he had me try the position of catcher. I remember him saying, "You're in control of the game. You have the ability to stop the game for a time out to talk to your pitcher, or another teammate. You call the pitches, and you give signals if you're going to throw someone out trying to steal second base. Take control. Your team trusts you. You've got this!"

So I did. I took control. I loved the feeling of being empowered, knowing my teammates trusted me to make the right call. I didn't have that kind of control in my life outside of sports. Having what seemed like a prestigious position on the field or on the court made things right with the world—at least for about two hours.

Freshman year of high school, after only a month of new classes, a sea of new faces, and a few basketball practices, I knew I'd be on the starting lineup doing what I loved. I was hopeful it would give me some instant friends, as my mother had said. She was right. I met some great friends on the basketball team. That was one of my most favorite basketball seasons, minus having to interact with a certain girl. Ravyn.

Rayvn decided on the same school I did. A summer of being apart didn't remove her distaste for me. Not much was said between us during the first few months of school, but once basketball season started, we were forced to be together for practices and games. Our relationship was okay at best before she realized I'd begun to make friends with some of the other girls. She noticed that some of the "jock" boys were starting to pay attention to me too. With her nose snarled up and her chin tucked in, she'd pivot and storm off. Ravyn started to spread rumors about me with the upperclassmen and anyone else that would listen.

Sitting in the bleachers watching the varsity girls basketball game, a jagged little rumor made it to my ears. Apparently, it was about me having done a very sexually mature act to a boy that I had genuinely never heard of before. I was upset and teary eyed, trying to hold back so everyone didn't see me cry. A group of senior boys began to turn around from their seats below, whispering, giving me the eye, and laughing. A few minutes later, one of the upperclassmen came up to me and asked.

"What's wrong? Why are you upset?"

"Ravyn has been telling her brother's friends that I did something really dirty, and I don't even know what that means.

My explanation struck a chord with him: "Don't worry about her. She's full of hot air and no one believes anything she says anyway. Are you gonna be okay?"

He smiled a Nick Newman kind of smile, and I nodded yes.

The first year of high school was like walking into a fall fair with lots of bright lights, dinging bells, people talking, laughing, and then ending up in the eerily lit spook house. It was exciting, nerve racking, scary, and like a whole new world. I met a really great group of girls that ranged from band members, cheerleaders, athletes, and academics. Out of a group of twelve, I became extremely close with two of them. I knew I could trust them because they were always there for me, and they didn't gossip about others. They had good hearts and were consistent in their friendships. We were all different, had different upbringings, came from different socioeconomic backgrounds, and were in different extracurricular activities. But those things were irrelevant. With Dawn being away at a different school, I didn't get to see her as often.

Confrontations with Ravyn miraculously ended for me after the first evening that I was asked to play "up" and mostly ride the bench for the girls junior varsity basketball team. I was over the moon excited. I was happy to be on the bench cheering on our teammates. Ravyn was sitting right next to me and made a poor decision to heckle our more seasoned players from the bench, shouting her opinions about their lack of hustle or creating a turnover. Right after the game, she was stopped short by one of those players and proceeded to get into a fistfight in the middle of the school cafeteria. Ravyn was expelled and I didn't see her after that, other than the rare appearance at a football game. Life was much easier without worrying about what she was going to say about me next, but as I look back on that now, I wonder what kind of devils she fought in her own life.

As I moved through tenth and eleventh grade, I became a bit more comfortable in my own skin. During my eleventh-grade basketball season, we got a new coach. She was not a fan of me. I wanted everyone to like me, and the thick cloud of pressure that came with varsity sports was an added stress. I fought hard for my position, but no amount of determination and will would convince her to give me a chance. I quit mid-season, which was one of the hardest decisions I had to make that year. It was like a part of me had died. So much of my character was tied to playing basketball, I wasn't sure what to do with myself. I thought my confidence might never heal until one day I was sleepily looking up answers to my history chapter lesson when my teacher, Coach Bull, interjected into the quiet. "Hey Andi, are you busy after school?"

After the initial shock of being jolted back to reality by his booming voice in a room with an echo, I said, "Yes, coach. Why?"

"I want you to come out and practice with us after school." Confused, I looked around at a few other classmates, and said, "Aren't you the tennis coach?"

"Yeah. So?"

Not being sixteen yet, I couldn't use a job as an excuse for why I couldn't come, so I began to give an account of all of the reasons I shouldn't or couldn't play.

"I've never played tennis a day in my life." I declared.

His rebuttal: "That's okay, I've seen you play ball. You're athletic and you can do it."

"I don't own a racket."

"I have an extra one I'll loan ya."

Lacking a further deterrent, I agreed and met up with everyone after school that day and had my first tennis practice. I knew nothing about the scoring, the rules, etcetera. Literally nothing about the sport was familiar to me. However, coach's faith in me was all it took to fuel my fire to be good at something again. I dove headfirst into the sport and played doubles and singles. I enjoyed the teamwork of playing doubles and how two people can be strongly in sync. My enjoyment of playing singles stemmed from being able to have faith in myself and telling myself I could do it and rooting myself on. We didn't play with an official line judge unless we were in the finals of a tournament, so it was up to the two players to be honest and work through any disagreements. I learned I could depend on myself. I was not a weak little girl, and I was capable of more than one thing. My doubles partner and I ended up playing a barn burner of a finals match in the regional tournament, and it qualified us to go to the state tournament that year.

The tournament was about an hour and a half away, so we had rooms at a hotel near the sports complex. This was the first time in athletics I stayed overnight for a tournament. The weekend of the tournament was my sixteenth birthday. I had a new boyfriend and he sent me the most beautiful arrangement of red roses to my room. I fell hard for that one. We dated for nine months and were together nearly every day. He drove thirty minutes round trip to pick me up for school and take me home before I got my license.

But then things took a turn, which in retrospect I suppose are destined to happen at such a young age. I was sixteen and had taken a job as a clerk at an old-fashioned drugstore on Main Street in my high school town. I was planning our prom attire in a daydream when I glanced out the windows at the front of the store. There he was, driving by, with his ex-girlfriend sitting right next to him in his truck. He must have forgotten to inform me we had broken up. I cried daily for six months into my senior year.

Again, those feelings of worthlessness crept back up into my daily life. Most of my friends had met their high school sweethearts during our junior year. While they were all "coupled up," and I felt like a foreign object. They still included me in gatherings, parties, or trips to the movies, and at this point I became more daring. I needed to feel something, like the way it felt to be pursued again, but now it was pushing the boundary up to getting in trouble.

I missed a lot of school in those days. I never favored the education portion of school, with exception for English and literature. Creative writing was my favorite. The place I could truly feel whatever emotion I was experiencing was when I sat in my bedroom floor, leaned against my bed with the radio playing, and wrote poems and song lyrics. Sometimes the music would give me clarity, and other times I could get lost in it. It was nearing graduation and I was doing a lot of reflecting. *Now what do I do?* All my friends had already been accepted to colleges, most with scholarships, and I had no clue what I wanted to do. I was grateful high school was coming to an end. I had no intention of going to college, and with no desire to return to a classroom, I decided to work for a while and figure out what I wanted to do when I grew up.

By the time I turned eighteen, I had floated from job to job and boyfriend to boyfriend. I felt like I was missing something. I couldn't figure out what I truly needed. Any shred of light in my life relied on wherever the party was, wherever I was included, or where I could feel a sense of belonging. I moved out of my parents' house for a whole month, only fifteen minutes away. I partied and worked and slept very little during those thirty days. By day thirty-one, I moved back home and felt like I slept for another thirty days.

At a wedding about three months later, I saw a friend's older brother. He was with another young woman who had a toddler girl. He looked happier than I'd ever seen him. I used to be really close friends with his sister and always knew he had a crush on me. I saw him outside as I was walking to my car to leave, it was dark out, and I had embraced a goth style. My hair was black, as were my fingernails; my highly inappropriate shirt and pleated skirt for a church wedding couldn't have been more of a sign I was "going through something." He started to ask about how I'd been and commented on how different but still beautiful I looked. I asked just enough questions to figure out the players in this chess match. I knew he was interested, but he was living in another state and relationships were already hard enough for me to stay engaged in before getting bored and moving on. He told me a month later he was moving back home because he wanted me. *He wanted me.* The day he moved back it felt like he'd been deployed in a faraway land and just returned home from active duty. He wasn't even in the military. Dopamine and the other euphoria-enhancing hormones distorted my vision and clarity, and we had sex.

But my head came out of the clouds the night of a party we went to with one of my girlfriends. He was driving us down a hill paved with gravel going too fast, fishtailing the back end of his short, wide truck. I was screaming, "Stop this truck and let us out if you're gonna drive like that!"

After repeated attempts to get him to stop the truck, we finally reached our destination. I got out of the truck, slammed the door, and marched into my parents' home without so much as a peep. We didn't speak for two months after that night.

A bit after my nineteenth birthday, I felt off. I also had not had my period in over two months.

I drove to a store thirty minutes from my home, bought a pregnancy test, and took it with me to a Taco Bell in the parking lot of the grocery store. I went into the bathroom that was dirty and smelled of urine mixed with fast food. It was only a one-person bathroom, so I locked the door and prayed no one would need to come in while I took the test. I was terrified I'd get caught with a pregnancy test and for the results themselves. I went to great lengths to keep this secret. After waiting for what seemed like an hour, sweat soaking the armpits and spine of my shirt, heart racing, it registered. Positive. I was pregnant and I'd only been with my friend's brother. On the drive home, this internal dialogue kept running through my head,

How am I going to explain this? I'm going to be a single mother. What do I do?

I was crying so hard I could barely breathe and was scared to death. I called one of my best friends. I'd forgotten that she'd just had a minor surgery that day and when her mom answered, she said she was still out of it from anesthesia and couldn't talk. *What are Mom and Dad going to say?* Fearful they would be mad, I waited for only a few hours before telling my mother because I couldn't keep the secret any longer. She handled it very well. She was supportive, helpful, and encouraging as always. I begged her to tell my dad for me, because I was too scared to do it. I never wanted to disappoint my parents. They were always at my sporting events, spelling bees, and band concerts to support me. My dad and I worked for the same company at the time.

About a week after telling my mom, Dad asked me to go out to lunch with him one day. He fessed up that mom had told him about the pregnancy and told me he loved me and would support me no matter what I decided to do.

He said, "You'll always be my little girl, even if you're having one of your own. I will always love you no matter what and just want you to be happy."

I was relieved, briefly. Then came the first-ever OB-GYN appointment. My mom helped me set it up with her doctor, the same one that delivered my three younger siblings. When it came time for the appointment, they told me they'd transferred my file over to the doctor's son. I went in, with Mom in tow. I did not like needles, having blood drawn, or who knows what else this doctor was going to have to do for the exam. I'd never been to this kind of doctor, so I was completely ignorant about what happened at these types of appointments.

"Feet in the stirrups and move your behind to the edge of the table please," said my new doctor.

There was an intense bright light on a swivel arm that he moved directly to my nether regions. It was so bright; I could feel the heat. None of my girlfriends had ever described this before, neither had the women in my family. I had nothing to compare it to in my imagination. It was humiliating and the most jolting reality check I'd had up to this point.

Ugh, this is mortifying. How is this real life? That test I took had to be wrong. I cannot do this. I can't be pregnant!

In order to be sure, the nurse asked me to dress then go into a private bathroom and pee in a cup.

After the exam and urinating into a cup while trying not to do so all over my hand while hovering over the toilet seat, I walked into my doctor's formal office. I felt like I was having an out-of-body experience. It felt like I was under water hearing my mom and the doctor talk. Even more, it was an inner body experience. The voice that was clear was the voice in my head that kept loudly blurting out whatever it damn well pleased. *What am I going to do? This can't be happening. I'm going to wake up tomorrow and this will have all been a dream.*

That day never came. I was pregnant, unmarried, and living with my parents with no idea of what I wanted my life to be. I didn't know who I truly was at my core or what was about to happen to me. What's more, being an unwed pregnant young woman took me to the top of the gossip mill in town. I heard from friends and my parents, by way of their friends, that others were talking about the biggest news to hit my small town since the oil boom. I cried myself to sleep many nights, praying I would be a good mother for this precious baby. That was now my only focus.

I started to realize this baby gave me purpose. The day I went for my ultrasound to find out the sex, my mom was with me. The doctor said, "Congratulations, it's a girl!"

I thanked God for sending this sweet baby girl to save me from myself. There's no telling what kind of trouble I would have gotten into had I not been blessed with her. She gave me a reason to get out of bed in the morning. The only reason I needed. She was the purest form of light amid my darkness. I was motivated to start planning how to care for this tiny human on my own. I wanted to be an independent single mother and didn't want to live with my parents forever. I had young siblings and my parents had their hands full. Another unexpected twist was my mother finding out she was pregnant about six weeks after my first doctor appointment. My mom and I were pregnant at the same time, two months apart. I was going to be a new mother; my mom was going to be a new grandmother and soon-to-be a mother of four. It ended up being such a cool experience to go through with my mom. She was seven months pregnant when I was induced.

Both of my parents and one of my best friends from high school were in the delivery room with me the entire time. The nurses would come in, do a double take of my mom, and look at me in the hospital bed with a perplexed expression. In my labor pain mentality, I quickly learned to explain, "Yes, that is my mom, she is only seven months along, just focus on me."

Mom and my friend voted for Dad to stay in the room with me while I got my epidural. That needle is about twelve inches long. The anesthesiologist asked me to lie on my side and curl in a ball. That's a feat when you're nine-plus months pregnant with giant belly and in pain. The doctor asked Dad to hold me still and he was face first in the action of the administration of the medication. He's a real trooper. I can only imagine it must have been difficult for him to watch his baby girl go through that kind of pain. After my daughter was born, it was all worth it. Every second of crying, the anxiousness, the pain of labor, and our unknown future were all forgotten for the first forty-eight hours. Clarity in the moment was intense. She would always be my little girl.

Reality soon set in like a record skipping and repeating the same three seconds of a song. I thought, *God, please help me take care of this angel!*

CHAPTER 4

THE DARKNESS REVEALED

———

I signed up for government assistance soon after I had my daughter, until I could find a job. I still had a car payment, insurance, food, diapers, and a cell phone to pay for. It was one of the most humbling experiences I've ever gone through. My family had never asked for money. Instead, they worked their tails off. My work ethic was strong, instilled by my parents, and I believed you *needed* to earn your money. It was important to me to pay for what I needed. I felt ashamed that I had to ask for financial help. Most importantly, I had to provide for her until I found a job. I already had feelings of being a failure as a mother to my one-month-old daughter.

Some months later, I took a job working at a business my cousin started about thirty minutes from home. I took my daughter to work with me, with a playpen and all the loot it takes to travel with a baby for nine hours. We went to work together Monday through Saturday from 10 a.m. to 6 p.m. It was the best scenario I could've hoped for. I couldn't imagine leaving her all day with someone else besides a family member.

At about the time she was six months old, she needed room to move. It was no longer realistic for me to take her with me. The storefront was small, and I felt guilty for having her there through the long workday. So, I hired a sitter. My first childhood sitter's daughter was my baby girl's first babysitter. I'd take my daughter by her home every morning and feel guilty all day. I knew she was being well cared for. Still, I felt an overwhelming sadness driving away.

After about a year in that job, a close friend of my dad's told me about a position open with his employer. After some typing tests and interviews, I secured the position that would propel me into the corporate world. That's where I met my first husband.

Until then, I had found nearly all the wrong men in a thirty-mile radius of home. My first husband, Chevy, was kind, thoughtful, and caring. We didn't date long before we were engaged and married. I was twenty-three at the time. He surprised me by buying a brand-new home for us. I was elated and couldn't believe the positive things that were happening in our lives.

Chevy was unbelievably good to my daughter and me. I could always count on him. He was eleven years older than me. I was immature in comparison. He had a college degree and a promising career, but even more he loved both of us unconditionally. Chevy and I were pregnant with our son in about six months of marriage. From the beginning, Chevy treated my daughter like his biological child. Most people assumed he was her father. He helped coach her softball and basketball teams and helped provide a safe, loving, and fun home for all of us.

Six months after my daughter turned five, she started kindergarten. Her brother was seven months old. It was an exciting time! She and I got to go shopping together for her new clothes, backpack, and school supplies. This was something I always looked forward to with my mother before the beginning of each school year and wanted to continue the tradition with my children.

When she started school, I began to get very anxious before dropping her off each morning. Eventually it got so bad I'd call a friend to come by and pick up my daughter to drop her off at school along with her daughter who was the same age. At first it was only a day or two a week, and then it became daily. It wasn't apparent to me that I needed professional help. I would get in the car to take her to school, and a heat would come over my face and chest. My heart would beat until I thought it would explode. My vision was affected, like my peripherals were covered with black fuzz. All these physiological feelings happened within fifteen to twenty seconds. My brain was in panic mode. Fight or flight?

What's happening to me? What's going on? What is WRONG with me? I'd repeat in my head.

Finally, I asked my mother to take me to a therapist. I thought a professional might be able to help me figure out why I was suddenly dealing with panic attacks. My mother planned to drive me to the appointment about forty-five minutes away from my home, my eight-month-old in tow. We hadn't gotten out of our neighborhood before the panic feelings started, with new symptoms of nausea, shaking, and weakness. I told my mom, "Turn around, I can't do this. Just take me back home."

She told me I could handle this and reassured me she would be right there with me.

I had always felt safe with my mom. Her uplifting words didn't keep the panic feelings away though. While she drove,

I had both hands gripped onto the seat so tightly my knuckles were turning white. I rode the whole way to the appointment that way. As soon as I walked into the office, I went straight to the bathroom. The profuse sweating began, I was visibly shaking, and I was sick to my stomach. I constantly fanned myself, trying to calm down, but I didn't know how. My body was taking over, and my mind couldn't turn it off. I couldn't find the STOP button.

I went into my therapy session after about fifteen minutes, but it seemed like an hour. My therapist spoke gently and had a soothing environment in her office: dark gray-green walls, soft light from a couple of small desk lamps lit the room, and a medium sized saltwater fish tank. There was a couch, two small recliners, and a coffee table in between the couch and chairs. There was a calm, pale yellow lab that lay lazily at her feet. She asked me a few questions I don't recall. Her questions, audibly, couldn't compare to my panic voice in my head screaming, *Danger! Danger! Danger!*

She asked me if she could try something with me, a different kind of therapy that may help me. I agreed in desperation for relief. She got on her knees on the floor, just in front of me while I sat on the couch. I typically avoided other people touching me, but I allowed it. My therapist asked me if she could touch my feet. I thought, *This is weird, lady, but you can do whatever it takes to fix me. Please just stop this madness.*

It was still hot and humid in Oklahoma, so I had sandals on. I took my sandals off and sat back against the couch. She was kneeling in front of me. She put each of my heels on either thigh. She said,

"I want you to close your eyes and clear your mind of everything else. I want you to only focus on the worst memory you have. Simply focus on that memory."

She began to alternate pushing her thumb into the pads of my feet. Left, right. Left, right, in a rhythm. About thirty seconds into this repetitive, alternating action, in my mind, I started to see what I can only explain as flashes of a movie scene being played in fast forward. It was horrible. It felt like I was five again. I'm not sure how long the therapy went on, but it couldn't have been more than forty-five seconds. Her voice brought me back. She said, "Andi, what did you see?"

I opened my eyes and realized I had both fists buried next to me on the couch and had pushed so hard I'd lifted my butt nearly completely off the couch. I must've looked like I'd seen a ghost, because when I made eye contact with my therapist, she said, "You are safe. Tell me what you saw."

I shook my head no, like a toddler being force-fed vegetables, all the while pushing my back as hard as I could into the back of the couch. My brain couldn't make sense of what had just occurred. She kept repeating to me that I was safe and encouraging me to tell her what I saw. She explained that anything I said to her would never leave that room, by law.

Continually, I shook my head no, but then I finally muttered, "I can't. I can't say it."

A few moments later, after she backed up and stopped touching my feet, I decided getting to the bottom of things was more important than my fear, so I told her about the memories I saw. She asked me how old I was when it happened to me. I answered, "Five. I was five years old."

Then, as if she already knew the answer, she asked, "And how old is your daughter?"

My mouth gaped open and my eyes wide, I said, "She's five."

She didn't say a word. She simply pursed her lips together and to one side, with raised eyebrows, and shook her head yes.

Lightbulb moment. I asked her a rhetorical question. "So, you're telling me because that happened to me when I was five and now my daughter is five, my brain is warning me?"

Again, she slowly nodded her head yes in agreement.

Whoa. The darkness I'd felt inside all those years was unexplained. I thought it was normal and everyone must feel that way and wondered if I just wasn't good at hiding it. Until that moment, at age twenty-five, sitting in my therapist's office I had no clue that the sexual abuse I endured from ages five to seven had any effect on me, my personality, my characteristics, my brain, or my fight-or-flight response. All the missing pieces about why I had certain worries, fears, and tendencies to want to control everything finally started to come into focus.

She explained the treatment she did on me was most commonly used on veterans of war that came home from deployment with PTSD. She said since it worked so well in that capacity, she wanted to try it with me. She said she thought I may have had a locked memory, and I needed to work through it. That was my first experience with EMDR therapy. It helped me process the memories that my five-year-old brain couldn't. Those memories had been ignored like smoldering coals for twenty years and now they had started a wildfire.

The memories of my sexual trauma were buried so deep, it was like I was watching an old movie in my mind that happened to somebody else. But I was one of the main characters in this film. During the treatment I could feel all the physiological feelings in my body, such as feeling nervous, scared, and intimidated, just like I was back in that tin shed with Jessica or locked in her bathroom. By the end of the therapy session, my level of anxiety went from a ten, or panic attack level, down to a one or two.

I thought because I was able to understand *why* these panic attacks were happening, I could move on and be "okay." Because I felt better immediately after the first therapy session, I thought I was healed. My takeaway, created by my imagination entirely, was that now I could move forward with my life like normal and be hypervigilant about who was around my daughter. Adult, child, family, or friend? Who it was had no relevance. I constantly questioned the motives of nearly everyone around her, regardless of if any reason was given for me to be skeptical.

Now that I remembered what I had buried eighteen to twenty years prior, I vowed never to tell my mother or my family. My therapist urged me to tell my mother. I explicitly told her that was never going to happen. It was done to ME by an older girl, not a member of my family or extended family. There was nothing anyone could do about it NOW. So, why would I tell my parents, grandparents, or anyone else? That would only cause them pain, sadness, grief, burden, guilt, or shame. I decided I'd carry those all on my own. I did tell my husband, Chevy, and eventually my two best friends since I had withdrawn for many weeks prior to therapy. I needed them to understand why I'd been distant and trusted them with my secret.

I didn't want to be viewed any differently by the people I loved. I still felt dirty, unclean, and shameful. So, I stuffed the memories back as far as I could. But when things got still and life was quiet, the memories would creep back in like a thief in the night, trying to steal my joy and murder my happiness. I figured out the busier I kept myself the less I had those memories resurface. It kept the darkness at bay. Not allowing myself time to think about the bad memories meant no panic attacks. I had to remain in control of my emotions, my surroundings, and my body.

Not long after, I learned I was wrong.

CHAPTER 5

ROLLER COASTERS

———

I've never been blindfolded on a roller coaster, but I have been on one inside a dark building. Part of the adrenaline rush was to create the absence of light. The passengers never knew which way the track was going to turn. Left or right? Up or down? My emotions mimicked that roller coaster in the dark. I loved my children. They were not the issue. I felt, and still feel, deep in my core they were blessings from God. I just happened to be on an emotional roller coaster of happy and sad. On this carnival ride, I was blindfolded. I never knew which way the track would turn.

In my early twenties, never having had the college experience nor venturing far from home, I didn't have much time to consider if I was "happy" or not. During the years my friends were in college, I was focused on taking care of my daughter, son, and working. Self-care wasn't a topic discussed in my neck of the woods. There wasn't a community of friends around me with similar lives to tell me I wasn't alone in the feelings I was having. I stayed busy, repainting one room at a time and redecorating, taking the kids to the park or my daughter's sporting events. The dark feelings stayed at bay if I stayed active, and I enjoyed working. I started to clean homes for extra money and eventually began my own professional residential and commercial cleaning company. At one point, I was cleaning two homes each day, five days a week.

I started to venture out by going to the gym after the kids' bedtime. Chevy stayed home. The kids were asleep, and I knew they were safe with Chevy, so I didn't feel as guilty. After working out I'd drive all over town, listening to the radio for an hour or more. I felt I needed *something* else. There was a piece missing. *Am I bored? There has to be more happiness in life than the way I feel.*

I built my cleaning business up to two or three homes per day, five days a week, and a commercial building on every other weekend. I had grown the business to the point of needing to hire help. I hired people, but the homeowners weren't pleased unless I did it, so one benefit of working so much was that I was in the best shape of my life, high school sports removed. Coming home on a Friday, after cleaning ten medium and large homes that week, I would drag myself out of the car and into the house from sheer exhaustion.

After three years, I burned myself out, so I decided to get back into the corporate world. A friend worked for a health insurance company and told me it was hiring. I started working for them in customer service, a call center, taking calls hopeful I would be able to help people. That was my assumption. And that assumption was wrong. After going through a rigorous six-week training, learning and testing on my knowledge of 350 medical terms, nine months into the job I was miserable. I would take naps in my car on my lunch hour. It was draining me emotionally and mentally. I couldn't sleep at night because I was dreading work the next day. I longed for the weekends, but by Sunday I was nauseous and anxious to go back to work. I felt like a caged animal—trapped.

After seeing me like this for weeks and being concerned, Chevy asked me one evening, "What do you really want to do for a living? What is that one thing that would make you happy? If you could choose any career, what would it be?"

"Hair!" I exclaimed.

That's what I wanted to be: a cosmetologist. He agreed to let me quit my job, pay for school, and have one income for ten months while I attended cosmetology school. I started working at a salon in our hometown and had a solid clientele built up within a year. I felt I'd finally found my calling. This new career made me feel needed. My clients loved me, and I had new referrals nearly every week. It was something I was really good at. Almost like sports in school, this was a way for me to stand out and be of value. So many other times I'd felt irrelevant and unnecessary.

About four months into being a full-time hairstylist, I started having feelings of dreading going home. I'd been married to Chevy for about seven years. I asked myself often, *Why is Chevy even with me? How can he be happy? We're nothing alike. I don't bring anything to this marriage. He's probably embarrassed of me at his family functions. I stick out like a sore thumb. I'm so different than everyone else.*

Chevy had quite a large family. He was one of four children and all of them had college degrees and a solid family structure. Chevy and I didn't fight. He typically gave in to whatever mood I was in at the time. We also grew apart through the years and didn't have much of a connection or relationship. I accept 90 percent blame for that. *Why was that?* I recalled my childhood, even into my early adulthood, my parents outwardly showed their affection to each other. They hugged in the kitchen, they joked with each other, and proved they were in it for the long haul. That was my definition of a good marriage, a successful marriage.

I was miserably unhappy. I thought, *Here we go again. What now?* It wasn't as if I didn't feel it coming on. What felt like an itch I couldn't reach to scratch, I'd go just a little further or do something a little more drastic each time I got antsy. There were missing pieces in my life I needed to get out and find. I worried I was giving our kids the wrong example of what a marriage should be. If I continued, it could ruin them for their adult relationships. We tried therapy to no avail. My mind was already made up. In my imagination, because I'd never seen him really angry, I worried he would hurt me if I told him I wanted a divorce. I planned my leaving for weeks. I met him at a therapy appointment, one Friday evening after work. I had it all mapped out. I was shaking when I told him during our session, "I want a divorce."

He looked perplexed and replied, "I don't know what to say. I'm in shock."

Every single second of it broke my heart. It was never his fault. It was all mine. I had hired an attorney, had the divorce papers drawn up, then asked a family friend to serve him after I was gone from the house, after telling him my intent.

It was an intense flood of emotions on the way home. We had a thirty-minute drive to get there, in separate cars, so that I could get my things and take our children to my parents' home for the weekend. My parents already had the kids, so I gathered enough for the weekend. I had already stored my keepsakes, for safety and even hid all the steak and butter knives as well as the pizza cutter. Since Chevy had always been so kind and easy to please, my imagination took over convincing me it would make the ten o'clock news: "A local forty-one-year-old man shot and killed his thirty-year-old wife in what seems was a domestic dispute . . ." the story fading into the background. Up to that point in my life, that had been the hardest decision I'd ever made. The divorce was more than hard. It was devastating. It was like mourning the loss of a loved one, except nobody died, and it was all my fault. He didn't deserve that. Upon reflection, I have regretted my behavior and can't help but wonder now if the feelings of being trapped and unsafe started nearly forty years earlier. It certainly did not come from the actions of Chevy. He'd never been aggressive toward me, yet I feared for my life by asking for a divorce at the risk of upsetting him. My imagination created this scene as if a monster persona was going to come out that I had never witnessed before. Memories of being held against my will by Jessica when I was a little girl and being terrified to displease her, which would lead to bad things happening to me, took over my rational thoughts at the time.

I chose to move out and let him keep the house. He did buy it before we were officially married, and it wasn't his decision to divorce. I felt guilty; he didn't deserve any of the pain I inflicted on him. I felt I let him and the children down. Obviously, making arrangements and moving into two separate households was much more extensive than letting him keep the house. I found a house that was up for sale but had been sitting on the market for a while. To help both of us, they offered to rent it to me. I moved in within a couple of days and it sold in the first month. *Are you kidding me? I have to move again?* We moved three times in that year during the divorce, which took eighteen months because I hired an attorney who ended up hitting on me, asking me out to dinner, and hijacking our lives for a year and a half. I fired him and represented myself in the end.

Enter guilt, sadness, shame, remorse, and more guilt. I tried to be the happiest, most attentive mom I could be while my children were with me. When they were gone to visit with their dads, I mostly cried, missed them, and became depressed. For many months, I got offers to go out with the girls on my off weekends. I just couldn't imagine going out. I thought I was ugly, used up, and worthless. *What man is going to want a divorcee with two kids from different dads?* After going through a well-masked depression for a year, I finally took my friends up on their offer. We went out to a country dance bar. It was fun! I wasn't home crying, mentally beating myself up for all the things I thought I'd done wrong in my adult life. Going out was fun for about six months. I still felt empty; something was still missing. I wondered if my friends were actually having fun or if they felt the same as me on the inside, going back home to an empty house. A brand-new roller coaster of emotions and various phases of light and darkness ensued.

No matter what I did, I couldn't find happiness. I never questioned why I was like this, or why I couldn't stick with anything—a man or a job—for very long. I must have looked like a whole conveyor belt full of baggage to the opposite sex.

Would anyone ever want me again? How do I achieve a happy life?

CHAPTER 6

NEW BEGINNINGS AND UNWANTED FEELINGS

———

I struggled to manage my depression after the divorce was finalized. Dating was harder than I'd remembered from my late teens and early twenties. I was tired of the less-than-desirable dates, interactions, and difficulties of dating in my early thirties. I wanted a partner, but because of the mental and emotional strain of the divorce and the dating pool being sparse—to put it kindly—I felt more and more negatively about myself. I appeared to be a hermit outside of my career. I needed to take time to work on myself, to heal. Six months after my divorce, I swore off dating.

Two days after my proclamation that I wasn't dating, I went out with friends for a birthday party. We'd planned to meet up for dinner then a dance club for her birthday festivities. We had a great dinner, and then we went to the dance club. It was packed! All my coworkers and their husbands were there. I was one of three single women in our party. We were dressed up, dancing, drinking a bit, and having fun. I excused myself to the restroom and when I returned, one of my coworkers elbowed me and said, "Hey, he was asking about you while you were gone."

"Who? Him?" I pointed to a muscular, tanned guy across the way. We were all standing in a large circle, as if someone was going to break into a dance in the middle.

"No! The guy next to him!"

"You mean the guy in the cowboy hat?"

"Yes."

I looked him up and down.

"Um, no. Doesn't he realize he's in a dance club? He's the only person in here dressed in Western clothes and boots."

I didn't have the best track record with cowboys in the past, so I wasn't interested in this one. He didn't seem to know that, continuously asking me to dance every time a new song came on. As the night went on, the cowboy asked for a fourth time and I agreed, reluctantly.

I thought I knew exactly who he would end up being. He'd be the typical player cowboy, looking for a one-night stand, and I'd never hear from him again. I wasn't taking the bait.

It was about midnight when a flurry of activity happened inside the club and people started pushing and shoving their way out and exiting the front door: a parking lot fight. Some of my friends' husbands were involved. I heard sirens in the distance, and like cockroaches scattering when you flip on the light, they were all gone. I turned around in a full circle looking for a familiar face. My friends all bolted before the cops arrived. I turned back around to go in and the only person I recognized was the cowboy. He said, "What happened? Did everyone leave you?"

With a smile, I shrugged my shoulders,

"It appears so, but I have my own car."

He invited me to come in and go out onto the patio to talk. The crowd had thinned, and it was much quieter. As we talked, we discovered we grew up in the same tiny town but didn't know each other because he was two years older, and his family moved to the town I went to high school in when he was a small child. We knew a lot of the same people.

I found out he'd been a bull rider for many years, beginning in his youth. He loved pretty much anything that most would consider an adrenaline rush. Something bordering on the edge of potential death? He was all in. It was nearing closing time, so I told him I was going to head home. He walked me to my car. He asked for my number, and we hugged goodbye. I was on the road for about ten minutes when he called. He asked if he could come by because we lived near each other. My children weren't home, so I agreed. I was still intentional about not sleeping with him. He stopped by and we stayed up until 6:30 a.m. talking, sharing large portions of our life histories, then falling asleep.

When we woke up the next morning, he asked if I wanted to go on a motorcycle ride with him and his friend. It was a beautiful sunny, spring Sunday, so we went. Under normal circumstances, I would have declined the offer and not put myself in a potentially dangerous situation. Riding a motorcycle with no helmet, I was thinking, *my mother would just die if she saw me right now.* We went by his friend's house to get him. It was the same guy from the night before. His friend had a comforting and uplifting way about him. He was always smiling, cracking a joke, and belly laughing. I felt comfortable with them, like I was protected.

The cowboy and I saw or spoke to each other every day after that. He was everything I thought I was missing—adventure, nearly zero fears—he thought I was beautiful and made sure I knew how he felt. He made me feel like the most special woman on the planet. We were both head over heels infatuated with each other. We couldn't find nearly enough time to be together. We dated for nine months, became engaged, and married one year and six days after the day we met. We had a connection like I'd not had with anyone else.

He had a son who was thirteen when we met, my daughter was then twelve, and my son was seven. I called his son my "bonus baby." All five of us moved into my childhood dream home, a two story, four-bedroom country-style home with a wraparound porch. Staying busy wasn't a problem, since each of our kids were in several sports throughout the year, in school and club ball. The first few years were literally a whirlwind of running kids to various events. I didn't feel that darkness anymore. Even though we lived paycheck to paycheck, we were happy. I was happy.

In our fifth year of marriage, I went through another phase of wanting something more out of my career. I left my cosmetology career and began in the staffing and recruiting industry. One of my best friends from high school, and the godmother to my daughter, worked for the staffing and recruiting firm, and she helped me get my foot in the door. I interviewed and got the job with no prior experience. My new corporate career was exciting! I finally felt important, needed, and relevant in my career. I made more money in the first year than I'd made in three years at another job. Six months into my new position, I was promoted to a manager role. I traveled about an hour and a half to a satellite office once a week to hire, train, go on sales calls, and do my best to be a good leader to promote them to success. My teams were like a second family to me. I truly loved each of them. I felt like I'd found my work home and a career that was meant for me, building relationships and helping others.

However, after three and a half years, I had no additional potential to promote and began to feel every day was Groundhog

Day. I felt stuck. Trapped. These feelings are what have always made me run before. *I can't leave. They've taught me everything I know about staffing, recruiting, and management.* I had only ever heard negative things about other staffing and recruitment firms from people in the company and other acquaintances in the industry. *Where would I even go?* I stayed put, which meant being unfulfilled and that old feeling of something being missing.

All these thoughts and feelings were on a subconscious level until one Sunday in January of 2014, on a free day, I took my sixteen-year-old daughter and nearly twelve-year-old son to go with me to the nail salon so my daughter and I could get our nails done, then go shopping and have a meal together. It was a sunny but chilly Sunday. My son sat waiting patiently, playing on my phone. We were all happy to have this special time together.

I had barely put my feet in the water of the pedicure chair when I started to feel nauseous and dizzy, and my vision became fuzzy. *No, not right now!* I thought. *I don't want to do this in front of my kids.*

I asked the pedicure tech to allow me to get my feet dried and did a fast walk to the bathroom. I was sweating profusely, my heart was racing, and I felt nauseous, like I was going to pass out. After about ten minutes, I regained my composure and came back out to the pedicure chair.

I put my feet in the water, and within fifteen seconds I felt it like an ocean wave crashing over me again.

I have to get out of here right now! It was the physiological feelings of a panic attack, but more intense than I'd ever had before. I couldn't talk myself through it this time. The tech said, "You okay? You look really pale."

I said, "I'm not feeling up to this right now. I'm just going to rest in the car while my daughter finishes her nails" and pointed at my daughter.

I promptly, in autopilot, dried my feet and threw my shoes on as quickly as possible. I asked my youngest son to come with me to the car and assured my daughter everything was fine, I just needed to lie down. I was not fine. I immediately took a drink of some type of soda I had in the cupholder, as it felt like I had low blood sugar from being so shaky and sweaty.

It had been quite some time since I last had a panic attack. I took a prescription anti-anxiety pill and put it under my tongue to dissolve it and get into my system faster. I was trying to figure out what this was, because this attack wasn't like the ones I'd had before. This was much more frightening, longer lasting, and uncontrollable. My son sat in the passenger seat of my car with me and said, "Mom are you going to be alright?"

I was laying back in the seat, on the driver's side facing away from him, shaking and sweaty. I told him, "Yes, I'll be fine honey. You are so sweet to be worried about me. My blood sugar is probably just low."

I turned on the air conditioner, even though it was quite cool outside since it was January. I called my husband to come pick me up. My son stayed behind and rode home with my daughter. I had never let my children see me go through a panic attack before and I felt guilty for worrying my children. Worrying them made me feel like a failure as a mother again.

My husband took me home. I felt better within an hour or so, but it took much longer for the physiological symptoms to go away this time. I came to the conclusion this episode might not have been a panic attack, so I took off work on Monday and got myself into my doctor for lab work and an office visit. I was able to drive myself there and back home without issue.

I went back to work on Tuesday and worked through Friday with no apparent issues. My lab results came back that

I was healthy as could be, except for a very low vitamin D level. The doctor said he thought I had a panic attack and that sometimes low levels of vitamin D, especially in the winter months because of lack of sunshine, can cause depression and anxiety. I started taking vitamin D daily, thinking that would fix the issue.

On Friday evening of the same week, my husband left to go out of state with our oldest son to a soccer tournament. I had planned a Friday movie night at home with my other two kids. I stopped and got some takeout on my way home. We ate and I started a fire and began a movie. I was lying on the couch and a tingling sensation started in my feet, like when your foot falls asleep, and then my heart started racing and I began to sweat and get cold. The cycle repeated for about ten minutes before I called my mother. I'd never had a panic attack while lying down before. I explained to her what was happening. My son and daughter were in the room, but it was like I was the only person in the room as I was hyperfocused on what might be happening to me.

My mom asked, "Honey, are you scared being out there alone, subconsciously, or do you think you're sick?

"I don't know what's wrong with me, but it's really scaring me and feels worse than a panic attack. Could you come out here? I need you here."

I was intensely frightened. I liked to be in control, and when I couldn't control the way my body was feeling, it felt like I was incapable of taking another breath. She said, "Of course, honey. I'll be there soon."

It wasn't fifteen minutes later my mom showed up with my maternal grandmother, whom we called Nana. They had a bag packed and offered to stay the night. Nana kept the two kids entertained, while my mom went with me to lie down on my bed. I had a large fan going and I was still sweating, then cold, shaking, and rubbing my feet together furiously in an attempt to make the tingling feeling go away. I couldn't do anything to counteract these feelings.

My mom lay in bed with me all night in her winter coat, because I was burning up and couldn't stand to have the heater on in the middle of winter. We checked, and I didn't have a fever. It felt like I was burning up from the inside out. I started to cry and grabbed her cold hand and thanked her for being with me and apologized for making her and Nana get out in the cold.

"I would rather freeze than not take care of you when you need me."

I lay there facing her, my eyes squeezed shut, holding her hand, and frantically rubbing my feet together for more than an hour before I was able to fall asleep. It was like I could feel every nerve in my body exposed through my skin. I thought this was how I was going to die. The next morning, my mom and Nana told the kids, "Go pack a bag, we are going to have a weekend sleepover!"

That Saturday was day one of being at my parents' for two weeks, in their den, in fetal position on her couch. I couldn't eat, and I barely wanted to drink anything. I wasn't able to eat a couple of saltine crackers or a few sips of soda at a time, and I don't recall eating anything more than that. Maybe I had some dry toast and water, but that was the extent of my diet for two weeks. My husband returned on that Sunday afternoon and came to get me to take me home and care for me. I didn't want to leave. This felt like my safe place for the time being. I just wanted my mom.

While staying at my parents' home, I cried in fear about an hour or two per day. I was scared because I couldn't control what was happening to me. I lay on the royal blue couch by the fire for hours, listening to the crackle of the fire and getting lost in watching the flames dance. Anything to avoid how awful I was feeling. I wasn't sure if I could be fixed and had thoughts that everything would be easier if I failed to exist anymore. I didn't know what to do to "fix" me. My mother took me into my primary doctor the next day. My husband met us there. I was so sick, weak, exhausted, and scared I couldn't even bear to sit up on the exam table. I lay down waiting for the doctor to come in. When he came in, he looked surprised as he'd just seen me a week before for lab work and thought it was a simple lack of vitamin D.

I told him the symptoms I'd been feeling and that I was scared. I started to cry, which isn't like me. I am typically very composed when under pressure or stress. He prescribed me Prozac. I took it for two days and it made me worse, so I declined taking more. Mom called the doctor and upon explanation he said to stop taking it and he prescribed another fast-acting anti-anxiety medication to get me back on my feet until they could find something that worked without the side effects. It worked quickly and I returned to work the following Monday. Life was back to my version of normal: staying as busy as possible. My work ethic was something I was proud of and partly responsible for my success in the staffing and recruiting industry. As long as I could keep those unwanted feelings from surfacing, I functioned like a machine at work.

In my personal life, I floated from season to season, year in and out, teetering between a mental break, running from my problems, and desperately wanting to find happiness, long-lasting happiness.

CHAPTER 7

CHASING THE PARTY

———

When my bonus boy graduated high school and went off to college, it was really strange: one fewer kid in the house. It was difficult to get used to jogging after running for five years. A year later, my daughter graduated high school and went off to college. Now we were at a fast walk versus jogging. About three months into having two fewer kids in the house, my husband and I really didn't know what to do with ourselves. I worried about my daughter daily. She was perfectly capable of being out on her own, but I injected my fears of the great big world into her situation. I faced the reality that the worry doesn't just disappear once children turn eighteen and spread their wings without you. It felt like someone took a part of my heart out and let it walk away. I had fixated myself on staying busy with my kids and my job for so long that I didn't know what to do with myself with spare time on my hands. My youngest son was with Chevy every other week, for the entire week. This meant every other week my cowboy and I were alone in the house.

We had a moment one weekend where we looked at each other and I said, "I feel like we're supposed to be somewhere. It's odd that we don't have a kid or two to run to a game or practice. Now what?"

We started to venture out, but most of our friends were all a bit younger and just starting to grow their families. We found a few new friends that were in a similar situation as us, somewhat empty nesters, or at least enough time to go out on the weekends. Those friends introduced us to more friends, and those friends to more. Our circle grew quickly within those few years. Our friends were from all different walks of life: some owned businesses, some were nurses, doctors, attorneys, blue-collar workers, real estate agents, and many other occupations. One thing we all had in common: we liked to have fun with no drama or judgement.

We went out and chased the party for years, along the way meeting new friends that we went off-roading and had pool parties with. There was always a birthday or anniversary party going on. I was always drinking no matter the gathering. I felt a sense of freedom with our new friends, but I was more fun when I was drinking. It took away the worried dialogue that was constantly in my head.

I'm not skinny enough. I'm not fun enough. I'm not pretty enough.

My inner voice was always comparing myself to anyone around me. I filtered myself by staying quiet and watching the crowd until I had enough alcohol to be social. The group seemed to enjoy me more when I was drinking, so that's what I did. I felt more included when I was drinking, acting free without a care in the world.

After a few years, I became so comfortable with our group of friends that I didn't feel like I had to impress anyone anymore; I'd just be myself. These friends gave me a freedom I hadn't felt since my friendship with Dawn. The more I acted like my carefree self, the more I got praise for it. By then, I was in my late thirties and about to turn forty. I dreaded my fortieth birthday. My friends came through and gave me the best surprise party. I ended up loving my fortieth and still feel like that was one of the best birthdays since childhood. I was so grateful for these friends, because I could tell them anything without judgement and be who I truly was around them. They supported me and allowed me to no longer live in a state of comparison or fear I was not good enough.

By this time, I was working for a new staffing and recruiting firm and was making even more money than I'd ever made previously. It wasn't difficult to pay the bills. We had extra money to do with what we wanted and a sense of security. We had started to meet some friends at the local casino on Wednesday nights and have dinner and a couple of drinks and play the card tables or machines afterward. Then we started to meet there a couple times a week with them or other friends. It was close entertainment since we lived out in the country. Before I knew it, I was going to the casino three to four times a week by myself and losing large sums of money. I started taking money from my joint accounts with my husband, ruining the financial stability we'd built up. I was consumed with guilt, but I couldn't stop. I also couldn't admit to myself that I was an addict.

When my husband first realized I might have an issue was the night I left our home around 10:30 p.m. to drive the twelve minutes to a nearby casino and play while he was asleep.

I'd been there about an hour when I was jolted back to reality by the sound of a familiar voice behind me, "What in the hell are you doing here?!"

I froze. It was my husband.

"Oh, well, um I just couldn't sleep and wanted to come and blow off some steam," I said, trying to stammer my way out of this predicament by lying.

He went on, "I've been calling your phone repeatedly for fifteen minutes or more. Now I know why you weren't answering," he said through gritted teeth.

"I swear I haven't gotten one call!" I said as I dug in my purse and pockets looking for my cell phone.

My phone was gone. I had laid it down on a machine somewhere on my journey to find the "big winning machine." He followed me to the players desk, a customer service desk where they take your information and give you a player's card to further track your playing time, your gambling totals, and your habits, times you visit, how long you play, etc. They had my phone; someone else found it and turned it in to lost and found. My husband stood right behind me, brows furrowed and looking like he might burst. I was humiliated because of my actions and for worrying him and scared because he was so pissed off.

We got outside and he simply said, "Get in your car and go straight home. We'll talk about this there."

"Shit! Shit! Shit!" I repeated once I got to the safety and privacy of my own car.

I had twelve minutes to think about what I was going to say to him to talk him into forgiving me. I felt I didn't deserve his forgiveness, but I wanted and needed it desperately. I'd never been a deceitful person and I still didn't understand why this gambling thing had such a death grip on me. When we arrived home, I recall sitting in the front porch light, sitting on a chair while he stood up across from me on the porch steps, thumbs tucked loosely in his front pockets and one knee bent and resting on the step railing. I feared he would leave me. I didn't want to lose him. I loved him, and I still do. He asked me why I left late at night without telling him where I was going. I had no good reason to give him. I told him the truth.

With tears streaming down my face, I explained, "It has a hold on me, and I have gotten us into a huge mess. It's all my fault and I'm sorry. We are behind on a bunch of our bills including our mortgage."

He was dumbfounded. He couldn't understand it.

"Can you promise me you'll stop now?"

I promised. I truly intended to keep it. And I broke that promise over and over and over again. I quit for a couple of weeks, but stress at work or elsewhere would trigger me to go back to a casino not near our house. I would go to the others that were further from home to continue to hide my addiction.

While waiting for the elevator doors to open in the underground parking garage, I'd see people exit the elevator looking irritated or sad, as if they'd lost and they were leaving. I thought to myself, *That's not going to be me, because I'm going to win!*

However, the house always wins. There may never be a truer statement. There were years I won between $20,000 and $55,000. I never walked away with a purse full of money because I always put it back into the machines, convinced I could win back all the money I'd ever lost at a casino.

Damn it. Why are you so fucking stupid? You are an embarrassment to how Mom and Dad raised you. You are such a fucking loser and a liar to the people that love you. You don't deserve to live.

This was my inner dialogue speaking directly to my ego after walking out of a casino binge with not a dollar in my pocket nor my account. Many times, this happened when I was in between paychecks, and I'd have to wait another week until payday.

The self-hate, feelings of worthlessness, pure heart-wrenching defeat, guilt, shame, and sadness came over me like a riptide. I dipped my toes in the water, felt fine, inched in little by little, was up to my knees, and before I knew I needed to scream for help I was swept underwater and being pulled away from the shoreline of safety by the undertow current. I have sat for ten hours at a time at a casino playing at one machine or bouncing around from one machine to another, depending on my luck and so-called intuition on which machine or bet would make me a winner and get me out of the hole I'd dug for myself. It was such a vicious cycle that felt uncontrollable. Looking back now, with not one ounce of desire to ever walk back into a casino, it still puzzles me how I fell victim to the allure and trap that is a gambling addiction. *Why couldn't I turn it off? Why couldn't I just stop?*

Traveling one floor up in a ridiculously slow elevator from the parking garage, the anticipation built: anticipation of what was to come during this visit and from scanning my surroundings for anyone that might know me. The doors slowly opened to what I interpreted as an adult's version of an amusement park or the state fair: enormously tall ceilings with massive geometric-shaped lighting fixtures in an array of blues, greens, pinks, and purples. There was a buzz and flurry of activity stepping off the elevator and onto the casino gaming floor. The music was audible, a mixture of seventies and eighties rock or chart-topping country, but it was almost an afterthought with the high amounts of distraction all around.

I entered the gaming floor, noticing a familiar and alluring scent. From my experience, each casino has its own distinct scent. If you blindfolded me and walked me into one of five casinos that I used to frequent, I'd test at one hundred percent based on sound and smell alone. It smells like a party or an exciting event that you don't need an invite to. Everyone eighteen years of age or older is welcomed with open arms and a "Hello, welcome to _____!"

Slot machines were my go-to; they mimicked video games from my childhood, only better. I had my favorite bays of machines I would play at each casino. I thought I had identified exactly which machines to play, that had the highest odds of paying out, and give me a way out of the financial mess I'd gotten myself into. They had graphics and specific noises that signaled no win and noises that were loud and distinct while the machine lit up brighter than a Christmas tree. This announced to the entire gaming floor that you'd hit a stroke of luck, which resulted in everyone within earshot instantly looking around for the flashing lights at the top, yet another demonstration of a win.

Like a pack of antelope in the Serengeti when a lion approaches, the crowd all raises their heads at attention. "Hitting" was the ultimate goal while playing slots. I waited with bated breath for my screen to light up red or give a sound that indicated impending free spins, which was a sign of possible jackpot or a significant win. People would start to walk over and monitor the situation, watching to see what my bet was, which machine I was playing, and how much I would win with those free spins. When I was on a hot run of free spins, curious people would gather behind me to see what I would win. This was both a high and a low. I was happy, but in my mind, I was thinking, *Be quiet, machine! This display is going to cause someone to see me, recognize me, and that will be the end of this escape!*

Other gamblers would hurry over in multiples, drinks and/or cigarettes in hand, to sit at a similar slot machine in the same bay and fervently slide their cash in the machine, in hopes of a similar result. This particular casino was one that most people in my circle of friends didn't frequent, except for special events like concerts or birthday parties—yet another safety measure on my part. I typically wouldn't visit the casino on nights they were having a live band or other events, for fear that someone I knew may be there and I'd be caught, and my husband could find out. If I happened to be there into the late evening by lying to my husband saying I had to work late or was otherwise busy with shopping, I would move from the bay of slot machines closest to the bar to another area further away from happy hour participants. I took even greater measures to avoid being spotted. I even tried to disguise myself by wearing a baseball cap or black clothing, nothing too bright or attractive.

I didn't notice this right away, but there are no windows or clocks in casinos. My guess is this is a strategic effort on the casinos' parts to create an environment that takes you entirely out of the "real" world and immerses you into theirs. The machines pulled me in and kept me engaged. I'd put my money in, hit the bet button, the reels would spin, and I'd sit with one hundred percent focus on the machine for any signal it was about to pay out. It was like I was hypnotized.

During the end of my gambling addiction, at its most destructive phase, I imagine I resembled a trained animal, sitting at a slot machine hitting the max bet button, awaiting a reward. I saw it. I felt it. I knew what I was doing was most certainly wrong, but I couldn't stop. I was conditioned by the strategy of these gaming machines. They are designed to give variable interval reinforcement of modest rewards. Even the payout lists at the top of most slots are a secondary conditioning measure to show me what I *could* win. While playing, the numerous smaller wins only encouraged me to keep playing. The frequent near wins, such as two of the three reels on pay line were frequent. Another near win, so my inner voice and sometimes audible whisper of a voice would say, *That was so close, I'm betting again,* and I'd sit in anticipation of a three- to five-second window to see if my bet had paid off.

Winning only instilled a stronger, more intense, draw to either keep playing or come back even more frequently. The way the games were designed reminded me of a popular movie, cartoon, or something that represents luck. The movies *Titanic* and *The Wizard of Oz* have games I've played, as well as Lucky Leprechaun. I was drawn to anything with 777, a typical number associated with good luck. Because the music or sounds of the machines were so distinct, I could hear something on television at home and it reminded me of a certain game. I played a game with an owl as the main character of the game. Every time I saw an owl in a picture, home décor, or anything really, it made me think of that game, which triggered me to think about that particular machine.

There were many of those games and triggers in daily life outside of the casino. I won't even go into the LED billboards or plain old paper billboards that announce how much a particular casino is giving away that month. I never even used my players card because I knew that is how they tracked how much you play, when you play, and how much you spend on any given visit. They say it's for rewards and free play money and comps for hotel rooms or dinner. I wasn't taking the risk of getting caught, because they also start mailing you their promotional offers, which would alert my husband I'd been going to the casino again.

The addiction, the pull, and the draw I felt to gambling and visiting the casino were all consuming. I had significant measures in place to keep track of my husband's whereabouts when I wanted to go to the casino. Another tactic of my attempt to get away with it.

I'd call him and say, "Hey, babe! How was your day? Do you have any plans for us this evening? I am going to be working late," or, "I'm going to run by the store on my way home and see if I can find (insert some random items here)." I'd use that excuse so I could say I went to the store, but they didn't have what I was looking for. I told lie, after lie, after lie to my husband, my children, my family, and my friends. *How am I going to get out of this mess?*

CHAPTER 8

A DEAL WITH THE DEVIL AND FINDING GOD

———

I had gotten us in such a financial choke hold that it seemed there was no way out. I borrowed money from friends, my family, and even took money out of my husband's nightstand he'd put back to save for a rainy day. I have gone so low as to put my own wedding ring on loan many times. I had to pay the amount I'd loaned against it before the due date or pay it and redo the loan the same day. Then I'd take the money and go straight back to the casino in hopes of winning to "get out of the hole." It felt like the was world closing in around me every time I went and lost hundreds, sometimes thousands of dollars. *How am I going to get out of this?*

One evening, after I'd nearly drained our accounts, my husband had discovered I'd been taking money out again after I'd promised not to. He had a come-to-Jesus talk with me. He seemed to be past the point of being angry and wanted to figure out a solution for us to recover financially. It was actually his idea to consider filing bankruptcy. I was so behind on house payments and various other bills that we decided to get a friend's opinion. We called a friend that night. He had been through a bankruptcy as well, and after filling him in on the amount we were behind, he encouraged us to go that route. We decided to contact an attorney and set up our consultation.

I had to face my addiction and admit why we were in this situation to the attorney and his assistant, all while my husband sat next to me: a humbling, scary, and nauseating experience. Now the legal field and government were going to be involved in my weekly life for eighteen months. The attorney and his assistant were amazing to work with. Yet I still remember the look on the assistant's face when I showed her our bank statements and totaled the amount I'd withdrawn at the casino over a six-month period, then over a year. She finally said, "Wow, you really had a problem. This is going to help you, but you have to stop going." I knew she was right, but it felt like I was making a deal with the devil.

Part of the process of starting the bankruptcy proceedings was going through all our bills, debt, and bank statements. The reality of the amount of money I'd thrown into slots hit me like a Mack Truck. I felt lower than I realized was ever possible. Because of our total compensation, our total income, we made too much for the type of bankruptcy in which the courts wipe the slate clean and allow you to start fresh. Instead, our bankruptcy was a Chapter 13 Full Repayment Plan. This means everyone we owed money to would be paid by the Chapter 13 Trustee's office by garnishing my paycheck every single week for eighteen months. The trustee garnished $665 each week and paid out a portion to each of the creditors we owed until everything was paid off. It doesn't sound like a long time when you read it, but when you're stuck on the merry-go-round for that long, it gets more dizzying and nauseating than imaginable. I felt like it would never end, while at the same time I was relieved and looking forward to turning things around and recovering. The good thing about this type of bankruptcy is that we paid off everything and owned it outright by the time it was over.

My husband stood by me, even after all the lies, deceit, and financial issues my addiction caused. He should have left me and would have been fully justified in doing so.

Because we didn't want to live out in the country anymore and didn't want to drag our bankruptcy out even longer, we let our house go up for auction versus putting it into the bankruptcy. My husband thought a change of scenery would do us good. We were in a different phase of our lives and were tired of living far from the city. We moved into an apartment my in-laws had to cosign for in the downtown area of a large city about thirty minutes away. About one year into the bankruptcy, I hit my mental and emotional rock bottom. The self-loathing and constantly berating myself was only adding to my downward spiral. I called my mother from a picnic table outside our apartment. It was dark outside, with the exception of a few streetlights scattered around the property.

I began by saying, "I need to say something to you and just need you to listen and understand I would never act on it. I am feeling such strong emotions of shame, guilt, and worthlessness. I think this world would be better without me in it."

My mother started to get choked up and began to cry through her words of encouragement. I reiterated that I wouldn't act on any suicidal thoughts because of the way she and my dad raised me. I couldn't do that to them, my husband, our children, or my friends. I just needed to vocalize it and get it out of my brain. We both cried a bit, but then she turned the conversation to focus my attention on all the positive things in my life.

I never shared that with my husband. I'm still not sure he realizes I felt unworthy of life. At the time, I couldn't put him through more than what he was already dealing with. Many times throughout the bankruptcy, if not for him, we would not have made it.

I stayed focused on work and staying busy, but I never really dealt with the problem. I still had fierce urges to go back to a casino. I would hear a certain sound that one of my favorite slot machines made and I could see the game in my mind. The images were so strong I thought, *I need to go back to the casino.* I fought it hard. At a certain point, I became so disgusted with the results of my addiction and what I had put our family through that I knew I had to do something to rewire my brain. I was in therapy a couple of different times with a psychiatrist and a therapist. Neither fully took the urges away. This was an addiction I had to overcome. I wasn't sure if I would ever stop having these thoughts and obsessing about the machines. I couldn't do it on my own and was too ashamed to go to a Gamblers Anonymous meeting.

My husband had already tried everything he knew to do. My mother had spoken with me many times, encouraging me to focus on a positive thing such as going back to working out, looking into new exercise classes, or making an appointment for a spa treatment once a week. My friends listened and did their best to be supportive, but at a certain point borrowing money became such common behavior they knew what I was up to. At this point in time, they didn't know what else to say to encourage me to fight the addiction, resist the urge to gamble. I was tired of being a burden on them.

I reached out to the only one I knew could help me. I asked God to forgive me and to help me through it, give me a distaste toward the casino, the games, and ever wanting to go back. I had been a Christian my entire life. I prayed for indifference frequently. After a few weeks of praying, a friend mentioned a church they followed online and suggested I listen in. I started listening to the church app replays of their sermons. Watching or listening to sermons became a survival tool for me. I listened to them while driving to work and home. Anytime I felt the urge, I looked up a new sermon by a different pastor and listened to it with headphones or through my car speakers to get the full effect of the worship music and sermons. I gave my life to God, again. I asked for His forgiveness and believed He had forgiven my sins. I never forgave myself though. I was still hanging onto the guilt and would beat myself up often. It was easier to believe God would forgive me than for me to convince myself I was worthy of forgiveness.

We were still living in the same apartment at the time our bankruptcy was discharged. I was sitting outside at night on a picnic table listening to a sermon when a thought came over me to check my email. I opened it and there was an email from my attorney's assistant with the subject line: "discharged." I thought I was hallucinating, somehow. I couldn't believe it was over. Finally! We made it! I ran upstairs and excitedly said to my husband, "Guess what! It's over! Our bankruptcy is paid off and it's over!" We came out debt free. The pressure of that money being withheld from my weekly check was over. Sweet relief. I could finally breathe again without worrying about money nearly every waking moment. It was a blessing in disguise, but not a free one. It cost us a lot. It cost me the trust of my husband. It cost me my reputation with family, friends, and others. I was glad the bankruptcy and addiction were over, but I still felt the guilt and immeasurable shame.

Two months later, I flew to my company's headquarters in Chicago. Management went there about twice a year for meetings. I flew out early in the morning. During my flight I reviewed my reports, made notes, and prepared for the presentation coming up the following day. When I arrived at the airport in Chicago, there were some familiar faces waiting on an Uber. I went outside for fresh air, while they waited inside the glass enclosure since it was still pretty cold for April in Chicago. We got in the car, I in the front seat and the other three in the back. It was about a twenty-minute drive in traffic to our hotel. While the ladies were in the backseat chatting, I remember looking at my phone to check emails and texts from my team back at the office. My vision started acting funny.

Even though it was overcast, I had my sunglasses on. I could see a kaleidoscope type of pattern in colors in all directions of my peripherals. I thought I'd looked down at my phone too long, so I didn't think much about it. When we arrived at the hotel, I was one of the first ones in and checked in. I went up to my room and as soon as the door shut behind me, it hit me. Panic, anxiety, and an overwhelming feeling of fear.

I put down my things and got my phone out to call my husband to help calm me down. When he answered, I could not speak. There was noise coming out, but I couldn't form words properly. Every word I said to him had an "ing" on the end of it. I panicked even more. I thought,

What is happening to me? Am I having a stroke?

He said, "Andi, take a deep breath. You're okay. What is going on? Where are you? Can you text one of your colleagues? I'll call the front desk to send help and call you right back.

All I could gather to say was "uh huh."

I tried to text my colleague, but all the words were jumbled, so I simply wrote, *325 Help*. I prayed she understood that meant my room number and I needed her.

My husband called me back. I was sitting on the edge of the bed. He said, "I called the front desk, and someone is coming up to check on you. Go ahead and lie on the bed with a pillow under your feet to elevate them."

I did as he said. I lay there listening to him to encourage me to breathe and telling me everything was going to be okay.

About the time I started to gain my composure, even though I was still trembling from the event that had just happened, there was a knock on the door. I got up, phone in hand, opened the door and saw my colleague and my boss. *How embarrassing!* I thought as I walked back to the bed and lay down. My husband asked me to hand the phone to my colleague. I could hear her and my husband talking about possibly calling an ambulance. I was screaming in my mind, *No, don't take me to the hospital in a city a million miles from my husband!*

Prior to hearing this I'd regained my ability to speak properly again. I assured them, "I'm fine now. I think I'm just tired and got overwhelmed. I'm just going to lie down and rest for a bit."

My husband stayed on the phone with me for a few more minutes, making small talk—his way of making sure I was okay and able to speak normally.

"I'll check in with you later this evening. Thank you for being there for me when I was scared and needed you."

Later that night, I met everyone out for happy hour and dinner. I started drinking and had enough to keep the worry thoughts at bay. That night I called my husband and let him know that I was fine now. I kept myself distracted from the lack of my husband by watching television before I went to sleep. I woke up the next morning, got ready, and met everyone downstairs to catch a ride to the office for a day of presentations. I didn't enjoy public speaking, at all, and I had to give my presentation to a group full of leaders that do the same job I do in a different city. I made it through the presentation. Thank God.

The second day was more presentations and meetings of the minds. I flew out that afternoon, made it back to my car at the airport, and was never so happy to be in familiar territory again. On my drive home to see my husband, I was grateful for the ability to do so, and witnessed a pretty amazing Oklahoma sunset. It felt like coming home after being gone for six months. I never wanted to leave his side again. I definitely didn't want whatever happened to me in Chicago to ever happen again. I thought, *You just got overwhelmed. You are intelligent. You did not have a stroke. It was a panic attack, just different than you've ever had before.*

I scheduled an optometrist appointment the day after I returned from my trip. Once I got to see my doctor, I told her what happened in Chicago. She examined my eyes. She asked me to explain again what I saw when we were in the Uber in Chicago. I explained the kaleidoscope type of colors in my peripherals. She pointed in the air, to signal she knew a possible reason for my distorted vision, and said, "I think I may know what that was. Let me show you something."

She went to her personal office and came back with a thick hardcover book, turned to a specific page, turned the book toward me, pointed at a picture, and asked, "Is this what you saw?"

"Yes! What does that mean? What is wrong with me?"

She explained that it was a symptom of an ocular migraine. I asked her what causes those, she said there were several variables. I asked her if she thought I had had a stroke. She said she didn't think so, but I should have an MRI to check for scar tissue, or it could've been a TIA (Transient Ischemic Attack), which won't show up on an exam.

Great. Now I have a whole new set of things to worry about.

Six months after the traumatic event in Chicago, in October 2018, I was let go from my full-time job. For reasons such as a nondisclosure agreement, I cannot share why I was let go. What I can say is that, based on the reason I was told, it was really nothing I had done wrong. People are let go often because of a clash of personalities or a difference of opinion. I had never been fired from a job since I started working at sixteen years old. I thought, *What am I going to do?* Our rent on the apartment was $1,330 a month and I wasn't sure what type of job I was going to land next. Since the next position I took was 1099 Contract, I didn't have health insurance, so my husband offered to carry me on his. I accepted much less money than I was used to making. The company had a good culture and had a refreshing vision at how to run a recruiting firm, so I was willing to take less money.

A few months in, we realized we couldn't afford to live in the apartment, so we decided to move into our RV for a few months to figure out where we wanted to start fresh and definitely for less than $1,330 per month. My wage had been cut from six figures to about a third of what I was used to earning. Had we not gone through the bankruptcy and the specific type we did, we wouldn't have been in such a good place financially for me to accept such a cut in pay.

Six months went by, and I realized this new position just wasn't a fit for me and what I wanted to do with my experience in the staffing industry. We parted ways on good terms. I began to work from home, supporting recruiting for a few clients.

Starting my own recruitment firm was something I said I never wanted to do. Yet, there I was, doing it on my own and only getting paid upon placing a direct hire candidate with a client. I continued to apply for other recruiting positions and interviewed several times from May to July 2019. Although the interviews went well, those doors were gently closed in July of 2019. After the last, "Thanks, but no thanks" call, I was sitting at my kitchen table in the RV, which also doubled as my desk. I hung up the phone and sat it down next to my laptop. I looked up at the ceiling and raised both hands straight up above me. What I said next came out without hesitation and unrehearsed.

I called out to Him, "Okay, God, I get the point. If you want me to start my own business I will. But I'm going to need your help and I also want a platform to share my story someday."

I looked back down at my laptop and got started. I jumped into the business and although it was months before I made a placement, I was successful. It was nerve racking not knowing when my next paycheck was coming in, so I worked for ten- to twelve-plus hours a day, even on the weekends. In my mind, this was a way to redeem myself for all the awfulness I'd put my husband through and prove to myself I could be a successful recruitment firm owner. Not once did my husband ever bring up the fact that I'd gotten us in this position, nor did he chastise me for our living in an RV. Again, it was his idea as a temporary solution. I was able to start my business with little overhead, trying daily to get my confidence and gain self-respect.

In the first quarter of 2020, less than a year after starting my own business, a global pandemic hit, and the country basically shut down for weeks upon weeks. Most of my clients were trying to set their employees up with equipment to work from home and navigating uncharted territory of the business world. There wasn't much business out there for me to get, but with a few core clients I was able to keep my business going. Five months into the pandemic, I found myself enjoying the isolation the pandemic brought about, as we were all told we were "safer at home."

In the past, when I was really struggling with panic, anxiety, or depression, my safe place was at home. I didn't notice it at first, but I really did feel safer at home, which was broadcast daily on the news and commercials in between shows since the virus was overtaking the globe. I worked remotely, from our RV, so I didn't leave much. With the exception of dropping off our laundry, picking up laundry, or curbside grocery pickup, I didn't leave home. The isolation only magnified my anxiety and panic. This was the perfect excuse for someone who wasn't healed and struggling in silence. It wasn't noticeable at first. It grew slowly, sneaking up on me like an invisible thief in the light of day, taking a small piece of my safety, comfort, and peace with each passing moment.

Once I noticed my anxiety and panic had returned, they began to grow more intense like a wildfire fueled by dry conditions and strong winds. *I cannot end up in bed for two weeks in fetal position like last time. What am I going to do if this business fails and I'm not making the kind of money I made before?* I would ask myself in a desperate attempt to avoid repeating the past.

CHAPTER 9

PANDEMIC, PANIC, AND FINDING GOD

———

The pressure began to mount the longer the pandemic went on. I was scared for a while that my business would fade away. I needed to do everything in my power to get new positions to fill, so I could earn a paycheck and keep my business going. The job market flooded with people who were laid off, furloughed, or unable to work because of the state or city mandates. It was like a feeding frenzy of people needing my help. I wanted to place every single one of them in a new and wonderful position and be the hero. However, the companies that were hiring would post the positions themselves and get 150-plus resumes for one job. They didn't need a recruiter, especially an outsourced recruiter who will charge a fee for finding their purple squirrels (a term meaning a hard-to-find, skilled candidate).

Another added issue around finding candidates for the few positions I had open was the number of people who weren't able to work. Thousands of families were affected by schools being closed and unemployment was keeping them afloat until schools reopened. My children were both grown; I worried about them regardless of their ability to care for themselves as adults. Not only was Oklahoma paying state unemployment benefits, but recipients also received an additional $600 for each week they filed. I joined several virtual calls a week to keep up with what was going on with new business and civil information. Regardless, I pushed forward with my business. It was a stressful, fear-filled, and depressing time for so many people. Others were doing home-improvement projects, investing in their lives, and taking road trips again. I was smack dab in the middle of those two worlds.

When I had the non-negotiable need to go into town to pick up my laundry or groceries, I would break out in a sweat, get nauseous, feel dizzy, or notice my vision was distorted. It mimicked vertigo. My trips were only five to six miles from home. I learned if I put an earbud in and listened to a sermon or a positive podcast about adversity and healing, the symptoms weren't as bad. I didn't play it through my car speakers because I needed to block out as much outside noise as possible. Outside stimuli wasn't helpful. If I didn't try to distract myself that way, my heart would start racing before I'd gotten a mile from home. I'd pick out what I was going to listen to and get it started before I even walked out my door to get in the car. I had to talk myself into going and would repeat many positive affirmations to myself as well as pray and pray some more.

"Lord Jesus, please be with me right now. Cover me. Put a hedge of protection around me, Lord.

"I am strong. I am loved. I am healthy. I am intelligent. I have the power to overcome obstacles." On and on I would go.

The more I listened to the positivity, the more I began to realize that I had to take my "fixing" into my own hands.

No one else could help me. I needed to seek help from a professional. I was ready to fight whatever was holding me back. I was exhausted from being so anxious and isolated. I dealt with these new, more intense symptoms for much longer than at the onset of the pandemic. I hadn't forgotten the episode in Chicago from two years prior. It popped up in my not-so-welcome memories often, especially when I felt overwhelmed. If I thought I might get overwhelmed in whatever scenario I could imagine, I avoided the activity or outing at all costs.

Part of the comfort level I found was sticking close to my husband if we left the house. My thoughts ran rampant: *What are we going to do all summer? We can't really go anywhere, travel, or do anything. Why don't we look into buying our own boat for this summer? That's one thing we can do together.*

We bought a boat in April 2020, at the onset of the pandemic, so we could at least have a peaceful retreat to go to on the weekends. That was our happy place. I loved being on the water; being in the sunshine helped my soul. The moonlight boat rides did me well too. The sunsets in between were something to marvel at; oranges, pinks, and purples covered the evening sky. The boat we bought was not a piddle-around-the-lake kind of boat. It was a power boat, and my husband loved it. It made me nervous, so I'd sit in the captain seat but swivel around with my feet on the back seat, watching the wake of the boat to keep from getting so scared.

Another trick I learned to avoid having the negative, worrisome thoughts was to drink heavily from about 12 p.m. to 1 a.m. on the weekends. I was still trying to control everything around me to avoid panic. The stronger my dependency on my husband grew and the more isolated I became during the weeks, the panic and anxiety started creeping up on me. I could do my job, run my business, and provide a great service to my clients and candidates. But I couldn't walk out to my car knowing I had to go to the gas station or through a drive-through without my heart racing, experiencing a hot flash, and get sweaty and dizzy. Feeling out of control over my own mind and body. Drinking heavily on the weekends was not a sustainable solution for my problems.

On a Saturday in June 2020, we tied up with a line of our friends' boats in a popular party cove of the lake. We'd been there a hundred times before over the past several years. Our boat was a speed boat and was much shorter than most of our friends' boats, which were cabin cruisers. We squeezed in between two of the bigger boats. After the flurry of activity of tying up and making sure all was secure, both my husband and I became hyper aware of the loud music. Loud music is one thing, but this was a stereo war between the boats on either side of us. It was loud enough to feel the vibration of the bass from either boat, playing two different songs. Immediately I thought, *Oh, this isn't going to work. This is too many stimuli. I'm going to get overwhelmed.*

Yet I used my inner voice and encouraged myself to go boat hop (walking across the backs of each boat) to say hello and visit with my friends. I went to a couple of boats and said hello, but I kept getting that feeling deep down that I couldn't stand still. I needed to keep moving. There were multiple conversations going on, loud so they could be heard over the blaring music. I decided I'd get in the water and talk to a couple of friends lying out on a mat behind the boats. The noise just reverberated off the water and right at me. Bad idea.

I tried to distract myself by talking to the girls, but every time I thought of a statement to interject into the conversation, I couldn't say it, or it was like a delayed reaction of what

I wanted to say taking too long to come out for it to make sense in the conversation. It felt like my brain was scrambled. Like the wires were all jumbled up. I swam back to my boat, climbed up the ladder, climbed over the backseat, and sat down. My husband was in our boat. He must've seen the look of fear in my eyes.

I signaled to him and mouthed the words, "I can't talk."

A little startled and confused, he asked me what was wrong.

All I could think of was to take one of my fast-acting anxiety pills. I focused really hard to say the words the right way.

"Red purse," I said and pointed to the cuddy cabin.

He grabbed my red purse, and I took a pill, drank some water, and looked up at him. I felt like my eyes were screaming, "Help me." Once again, he talked me through it. I lay across the back seat and propped my feet up on the edge of the boat, to keep them elevated. He was putting on a good face, smiling and talking with me about nothing. He was making small talk and trying to distract me from staying in my head too long. He'd ask a simple question that only required a "yes" or "no" answer every couple of minutes. About ten minutes later, he said, "Why don't we pull out of here and go for a slow cruise back to the campsite?"

I nodded my head in agreement. I always helped with untying, tossing ropes, etc., but this time I just sat there and let my husband and the guys from the boats beside us do the work to get us out of there. I didn't know if I could process a question and come up with an answer if someone were to approach me. I sat on the back bench seat staring at the floor of the boat until we were loose. I moved up to one of the single seats next to my husband. The whole boat ride back was about twenty minutes, I slowly spun the chair around to face backward, watching the shoreline and the wake. I was looking away from my husband and rehearsing the only thing I could control and manage, "Our Father, who art in heaven, hallowed be thy name. . . ."

I probably said the full prayer ten times. Then I'd pray for healing, restoration of my mind, and protection.

We got back to the dock, and I could speak one- or two-word answers, as my husband was testing me by continuing small talk. We got on our golf cart to head home. He headed to the bar to get a bag of ice, and after paying, he walked outside to get the bag of ice from the large silver chest. Out walked the bartender to say hello. I'd seen her at least fifty times before; we'd talked at length, and I'd been there every weekend from April to June thus far. I felt like my mind was in purgatory. The wires in my brain were still "untangling." I recognized the bartender, but I could not think of her name. I made very short small talk with her, mainly smiling and nodding, as my husband did most of the talking. Once we pulled away on the golf cart. I asked him slowly and intentionally, "What is her name? I can't remember. I know that I should know it, but I don't right now."

"Her name is Sunny," he said with a concerned look on his face.

"That doesn't seem right to me."

"Babe, we see her every weekend." He was still looking at me in a scared sort of disbelief that I really couldn't remember this piece of information.

The fact it didn't make sense that her name was Sunny made me start to panic again. *Was there something else medically wrong with me?*

CHAPTER 10

FINDING PEACE IN THE PIECES

———

I reached out to a friend that I knew saw a therapist/counselor at one point. She referred me to her counselor, who was certified in EMDR therapy. I called the counselor the same day and asked to get on her calendar as quickly as possible. I gave up a few years prior trying new anti-anxiety medications. I was even more aware that all the fear, guilt, shame, and secrets I'd held onto all of these years were not going away. They were getting worse. Either I became allergic to, or intolerant of, all anti-anxiety/depression medications. There were only two I hadn't tried. With a glimmer of hope this time might be different, my doctor prescribed one, and I took it for two days. On the third day I woke up at 4 a.m. feeling like my nerves were poking through my skin from head to toes. I lay in bed frantically rubbing my feet together and praying to God for it to stop.

The next morning, I called the doctor, and after hearing my symptoms, the doctor instructed me to stop taking the medication. That was good because I wasn't planning on taking it again. The same day, the doctor's office sent over the last drug on the list to the pharmacy. I filled it and sat it on my kitchen table. After three days, I sat with the bottle in my hand staring at it. I thought, *Should I take this or not? Maybe this is the one medication that will fix me.* After much discussion with myself, I couldn't bring myself to take it. I was fearful it would make me feel worse, just like all the others did, more so because I feared I would never truly heal if I masked the pain again. I was ready to do the work I knew it would take to heal from thirty-eight years' worth of unprocessed trauma. I had been to countless therapists, counselors, doctors, and even a psychiatrist. The counselor was booked out about two weeks from the day I called, and because we were in the middle of a pandemic, she was only seeing patients virtually.

My counselor had applied many times to be listed as a provider with my insurance company, but they denied her because they "already had too many providers in her area of experience within their network." So, I paid for every visit out of pocket because they denied my original claim. I filed three appeals with my insurance company for being unwilling to view it as an out-of-network visit. They denied me four times. In my opinion, based on experience, it is extremely disheartening that some insurance companies would rather pay for part of prescription and part of a doctor's visit co-pay to avoid paying part of a counselor's and therapist's fee for their hourly sessions. In experiences I have had with a couple, but not all, insurance companies, I have noticed they get their premium money every month, so it's no skin off their noses to deny me of this service. My point is mental health is important. I'll leave that be for now.

I decided to stop wasting my energy and focus on healing, rather than fighting the insurance company to help pay for a service I desperately needed. Regardless, I wanted to get better. I needed to get better! I was a fairly independent woman and it had been so long since I felt that independence. I felt I was becoming my husband's shadow again. I had to go everywhere he went or stay at home and isolate. It was getting annoying to him and me both. I didn't want to feel so scared at the thought of what may happen to me while he was gone. I'd even fight through the fears enough to go to a hardware store, at my husband's invitation, in order to keep him happy. I knew he'd protect me, save me, or help me out of a panic attack should anything happen. That didn't stop me from adjusting my glasses, cleaning them, putting on hand sanitizer, or literally anything to keep my mind occupied—busy.

What seemed like a month later—two weeks, in reality—I was able to see my counselor and get started. I was pushing off a panic attack on our first visit. I was even in the comfort of my own home in front of my laptop at my kitchen table. The first couple of sessions I mainly talked about my child-hood trauma and brought her up to date on the lowest of low points of my life—typical for the counselor to get to know you. I had been to at least ten between the ages of twenty-five and forty-four. This time I told her of the sexual abuse as a child, bullying, feelings of worthless, gambling addiction, bankruptcy, being fired for the first time in my life, and the panic and anxiety attacks. I was concerned she wouldn't be able to do the EMDR therapy, which seemed to work best for me, since we weren't in person. To my surprise, she was able to do the therapy virtually by sharing a link in the video chat.

She shared the link. I clicked on it and a white window that covered my screen appeared with a blue circle the size of a quarter in the middle. I could still hear her, she could

FINDING PEACE IN THE PIECES · 101

see and hear me, but I could only see the white screen with the blue circle.

She said, "Think of the worst memory you have. Focus on that memory in your mind's eye while you watch the blue ball bounce from side to side. Just watch the blue ball while you think of that memory. Do you have it?"

I said, "Yes."

She said, "Okay, here we go" in a soothing tone.

The first couple of twenty-second rounds, it was difficult for me to stay in the memory. Keeping that memory in front of my mind consistently: that's what I needed to do in order to process these memories and take away the physiological feelings attached to them. At the end of one round, she would stop the ball in the middle of the screen and ask me to take a deep breath in, hold, then let it out. She would ask,

"How did you feel?"

"I think the reason ..."

"No. Not what you thought. Tell me what you felt."

I was still trying to understand it and fix myself, even with her help. The desperate nature of my need to heal was frustrating. This process was not going to be a quick fix, in which, after six sessions, I'd be healed. It takes several rounds of EMDR therapy to process out the negative feelings related to each trauma. All trauma is different because we're all different. I never compare traumas but have heard them called big "T" trauma and little "t" traumas. Why would I compare my trauma to anyone else's? Everyone has a different experience. Yes, we have many similarities, but no two people will have the exact same experience.

She and I would process, via the white screen and blue ball, through a specific memory or traumatic event. I would choose a certain negative memory and it would take about four to six times before the feelings of panic, fear, shame, and/or guilt would leave me. One memory at a time, session by session, I started getting better. I got my independence back. I was standing on solid ground and my world wasn't spinning so fast anymore. I was able to drive to pick up laundry, groceries, then go into a store without feeling that heart racing, dizzy feeling. She gave me a few tests to determine if I had PTSD, based on how I rated my anxiety before the first session and five months into our sessions. She diagnosed me with PTSD, agoraphobic panic disorder, and generalized panic disorder.

"What does agoraphobic panic disorder mean?"

She answered in a much more educated way, but the way I interpreted it is being fearful and worrying about something that may happen to cause a panic attack. I thought if I could understand how my brain works, I'd be able to stop the fight-or-flight conditioned panic response by simply overpowering it. That is not how it went for me. Understanding the biology of how it happens does not prevent the panic attack from rearing its ugly head.

At the six-month mark in my therapy, I began to reflect on my progress. I wondered if there were others that dealt with the same things I had. I was curious to know if I was the only one that had been to counselor after counselor, only to end up at the doctor with a prescription tossed to them that didn't fix anything. Once I started to open up to people in my circle of friends about what I was going through, men and women of a wide age span of twenty-three to sixty-eight shared they had been through their own traumas and never truly recovered from them. They shared they felt it was too late. I waited thirty-eight years before I committed to fixing the root of the problem and moving forward from there. It took me two months of therapy to get to the point of finally divulging the childhood trauma to my mother. I had a peace I had never felt. A peace I found in the pieces.

By divine intervention and multiple confirmations, I knew I was being called to write a book about my life. I had asked God for a platform to share my story back in July 2019, and twelve months later, in July 2020 during a global pandemic, I got the call to write the book. For a span of several weeks, I received confirmation that I was supposed to write a book; every sermon I watched online, podcast I listened to, or other forms of media said, "Write the book" or "Start writing." Even the *Farmers' Almanac* had something called "best days" that I ran across that boldly said, "Write."

In late summer that year, while sitting on our golf cart at the lake looking out at the moon reflecting off the water, I blurted out to my husband, "I want to write a book."

He cocked his head at me and said, "A book?"

"Yes, I want to write a book."

"About what?"

"My life." I said with raised brows and a smile.

"What about your life?"

"My sexual abuse as a child, my struggles with panic and anxiety, my addiction, and how I finally found a way to heal."

We had a conversation about the topics that I felt I was supposed to share and asked him if he was comfortable with me telling my story. I explained that I wanted to empower other people who may be suffering from the same things. With some hesitancy, concerned for my well-being about what this might do to my mental health, he supported me.

I started writing.

The first bridge I needed to cross was telling my mother what happened to me as a little girl, yet again a suggestion from my counselor. So, I wrote the letter to my mother. I don't have many regrets in my life, but two of them left a mark: quitting basketball mid-season in high school and waiting until I was forty-three to tell my mother the truth. My viewpoint is that everything that happened to me was for a reason and part of a bigger picture. I believe God uses what was meant to cause us harm and turns it into something good. I have faith He is using my experience to speak to someone else who needs to know they are not alone; healing is possible, no matter how long the pain has been there.

I felt called to share what I've discovered thus far. As I continue to learn, I am realizing it's just the beginning of true healing for me.

Healing and finding peace is not a sprint, it's an unhurried journey worth every intense, frightening, beautiful, and triumphant step: a step I encourage others to take. One step in the right direction is one fewer taken in the wrong direction.

You have the power to live victoriously. I have faith in you. What will your first step be?

EPILOGUE

STARTING FROM SCRATCH

———

OCTOBER 2021

Sitting in my new apartment on my new couch with pink fluffy pillows, I stare at the cursor flashing on the white screen of my laptop, like a timer set as a reminder to write the end of this book. Filing through memories, I reflect of my transformation over the last fifteen months and daydream about what my future may hold. I realize, after glancing at the date on my laptop, it was one year ago this week when I called my mother to read her the letter.

My expedition fully began when I opened up to her. My counseling sessions from July to October 2020 helped prepare me for that conversation. I wasn't prepared for the feelings I would have in this moment: public display of my life in the pages. *How would people receive this message? Will they understand why I did things I'm not proud of? Will someone be encouraged by my story?* Some have asked me if I am writing this to position myself as a victim. The answer is no. I have never felt like a victim. I always thought there was something about me that caused the disgraceful actions of others. Now I know that isn't true.

My consciousness of my declining mental state a few months into the pandemic was considerably magnified. It took me hitting my version of mental rock bottom before I accepted the fact that no one was coming to save me. Neither my husband, family, nor friends could fix me. I didn't expect them to. I had leaned on them heavily until the revelation sunk in that they weren't trained professionals, and it wasn't in their power to bring me back to life, a life I'd dreamt of. Life with peace, love, and a courage devoid of irrational fears—that is what my heaven on earth looks like.

Starting from scratch has become a running theme since beginning therapy full time. The day after moving into my new place, at forty-four, I was baptized in a little church in my hometown by one of my dear childhood friends who had become the pastor—full-circle moment. People, memories, thoughts, and feelings had all come full circle back to me. This time they were all positive. When I came out of the water, I noticed such a peace in my spirit and a weightlessness that seems impossible to describe. I cried and wrapped my arms around the pastor's neck for longer than I presume he expected. Watching a video of the event and realistically having those emotions are two very different things.

A favorite quote of mine is by Mark Twain:

"The two most important days in your life are the day you are born and the day you find out why."

I have found my purpose.

I believe it is to encourage others who have been through traumatic things. To create healing change for those who have suffered or are suffering. To give people hope. I have faith in God that what was meant to destroy me will be used for good in the end.

It's quite a difficult thing to share the worst parts of you. Yet here we are, divinely initiated long ago.

This does not mean you have to be a Christian to receive healing, recovery, or hope. This is designed to be a lighthouse during someone's dark and intense storm.

I am not a trained mental health professional. I do have a story, much like many who will read it, and I pray it reaches anyone finding themselves in their own rock bottom.

My petition to those who have reached their bottom: Please. Don't. Give. Up.

Once you've reached the bottom, speaking from experience, I can say there truly is only one way out—up.

You can start from scratch too. You can have the life you've been dreaming about. You weren't meant to live a life on the bottom. Reach out to a professional for help and keep going until you're satisfied with where you are. You have the right to fight for your peace. It may not be easy, quick, or something you can control. By releasing control and accepting the help I needed, I am no longer ashamed or embarrassed by the happenings in my life. I am worthy. I am exactly where I need to be. Let me encourage you to keep dreaming of finding your balance and take action to bring it into your reality.

You deserve it.

Close your eyes. Envision what your peaceful life looks like. Imagine your best friend or favorite person is whispering these words to you.

You are worthy.

You are good.

You are loved.

You have value.

You deserve better.

You can do difficult things.

You have so much to offer the world.

Open your eyes. What do you see?

If you don't see the beautiful life that was in your mind, run.

But this time, run to chase down your missing pieces rather than running away from the truth.

As I adjust in my chair, I ask myself, *What now?*

A podcast, a children's book, or my next chapter?

Another missing piece I am ready to chase down.

RESOURCES

—

National Suicide Prevention Lifeline: **800-273-8255**

Lifeline (suicidepreventionlifeline.org)

RAINN, national sexual violence hotline: **800-656-4673**
www.rainn.org

National Problem Gambling Helpline Network:
800-522-4700 (call or text)

National Council on Problem Gambling:
www.ncpgambling.org

Substance Abuse and Mental Health Services Administration: **800-662-4357**
http://samhsa.gov/

Information for those who have suffered or are currently suffering from bullying: **800-273-8255**
http://stopbulling.com/

If you are experiencing a medical emergency, you are in danger, or feeling suicidal, call 911 immediately.

ACKNOWLEDGMENTS

———

First, I want to thank God, my parents, siblings, family, husband, my children, and my friends for never giving up on me and loving me through my good days and the bad ones.

Thank you to my counselor who helped me overcome my traumas and helped me realize I am exactly who I need to be and that is enough. "Ride the wave" is what I will continue to do.

I'd also like to thank my business and spiritual mentor, Rudy, as well as my book coach, Kim Spence-Mullen, who helped me start this book writing journey.

Shannon Rose Quist, thanks to you, whom, without our connecting via a mutual friend, I may have overlooked the program that catapulted this book into reality. Special thanks to Eric Koester, with the Creator Institute at Georgetown University, and all the wonderful staff that presented weekly Zoom calls to prepare and guide me through the journey that was writing this book.

To my sincere, kind, supportive, and knowledgeable marketing and revisions editor Julie—it's doubtful my blood, sweat, tears, and laughter would have made it onto the pages and to publication on time without you.

To all my family, friends, coworkers who became friends, and others I cannot mention by name for anonymity reasons—thank you! You each have your own story in my heart, and I'll always be grateful for each one of you.

To everyone who supported me before the book was completed by purchasing a copy, multiple copies, making monetary donations, and sharing my dream of reaching thousands (with hope for many more) with a message of hope—I am humbled and honored. You may have heard me tell a part of my story in person or in pictures on social media. My heartfelt thanks go out to each of you. If your name is not on this list, that doesn't mean that you weren't an integral part of one or more phases of my life. There are so many people who have come in and gone out of my life over forty-four years; it's simply impossible to name each one of you. Know your presence touched my life or taught me a lesson. All lessons learned are good ones, in my eyes, because they propel us forward into our calling. Again, thank you for all your support in my mission to create positive change.

Shanna Gore, Jordan Ask, Christyrae Looney, Amy Alonso, Stacy Gabriel, Jayme Lakey, Angela Wells, Janet Montez, Alecia Robinson, Kimberly Spence-Mullen, Gina Crase-Patterson, Melissa Pfeiffer, Sheila Hanes, Sonya Pyles, Dayton Crofut, Summer Dennett, Jim Hanchen, Nicole Lewis, Lisa McElroy, Jennifer Johnson, Andrea R., Janice Williams, Shirley Dennis, Machele Galloway, Sabrina Walden, Carol Robinson, Teresa Warner, Diana Humble, Jennifer Thomas, Rebekah Adams,Courtney Solorzano, Christina Kelley, Elizabeth Roark, Ricky Allen, Derrick Hardridge, Natalie Stockton, Brad O'Hara, Jami Robinson, Rebecca Pinkley, Shanna Alstead, Ryan Zilm, Sally Cryder, Gloria Hale, Jenni Jenkins, Brandy Wecker, Talitha Tiger, Amanda Stehle, CJ Jankas,

Tressa Selby, Emma Keller, Charles Morris, Jeni Morrow, Holly Crase, Jaime Westerman, Lisa Wilson, Vicky Brown, Shannon Quist, Rhiannon Baker, Cindy Montague, Shailee Patton, Jenny Sadler-Murphy, Joyce Roberts, Dawn Lanning, Carey Neely, Renea Gaskill, Sharon Rasberry, Shannon Rainwater, Vicki Jeffries, Vonda Basks, Rudy Upshaw, Traci Horner, Jonathon Campbell, Terri McCauley, Kellie Brown-Gee, Stacey Tarwater, Tiffany Taylor, Lauren Jones Cross, Lauren Cleary, Tonya Jarvis, Eusty Barbee, Julie Jennings, Mandie Joplin, Gretchen Gleason, Angela Gann, Heather Dysart, Courtney LaRae Holt, Nancy Deatherage, Tammy Payne, Victoria Myers, Marian Russell, Eric Koester, April Parker, Carol McNemar, Reagan Henderson, Lauren Osborn, Michele Burke, Tami Tarwater, Vicky Tarwater, Michelle Grigg, Jackie Lee, and Tiffany Bailey.

CPSIA information can be obtained
at www.ICGtesting.com
Printed in the USA
LVHW080801170422
716268LV00004B/89